THE JOURNEYMAN

Published in 1998 by Marino Books,
an imprint of Mercier Press
16 Hume Street Dublin 2
Tel: (01) 661 5299; Fax: (01) 661 8583
e.mail: books@marino.ie

This paperback edition 1999

Trade enquiries to CMD Distribution
55A Spruce Avenue
Stillorgan Industrial Estate
Blackrock County Dublin
Tel: (01) 294 2556; Fax: (01) 294 2564

© Éamon Kelly 1998

ISBN 1 86023 086 5
10 9 8 7 6 5 4 3 2 1
A CIP record for this title is available
from the British Library

Cover design by Penhouse Design
Set in Garamond Narrow (120%)11.5/15
Printed in Ireland by ColourBooks,
Baldoyle Industrial Estate, Dublin 13

THE JOURNEYMAN

ÉAMON KELLY

IRISH AMERICAN BOOK COMPANY (IABC)
BOULDER, COLORADO

For Eoin and Brian

CONTENTS

1

SEA SHANTIES,

SHAKESPEARE AND *POITÍN*

'Little paint and many waters!' the Dutch professor who gave occasional lessons on furniture design advised us when he wanted a transparent colour to wash over a pencil drawing. Mr Romein was a big man with large hands, yet with a few deft strokes of the brush he coloured in a sideboard or a Chesterfield suite in a jiffy. His English was as colourful as the paints he used, but he had a good sense of humour and smiled with us when he made a language blunder. One day as he came in and found us in a merry mood in the classroom I saw him cry.

'How can you laugh, gentlemen,' he said, 'when my country was invaded by Germany this morning!'

We calmed him down and said we were sorry. To see this huge man so distressed had a sobering effect on us. His tears brought me back to the time when as small children we dived under the table at night when we heard the Tan lorries approaching. I could visualise the German tanks thundering over the Dutch border and people who yesterday were free now looking for some place to hide. I was twelve months in Dublin and the Second World War was raging. The windows of the College of Art, where we were housed, had had dark blue shades recently fitted and these were drawn when darkness fell, so that no light filtered through to the sky to tempt the Nazi warplanes to release their deadly cargo — as they did later on the city's North Strand.

There were twenty of us, trainee woodwork teachers on a course in the National College of Art which was situated between Leinster House and the National Library. Military stood sentry by the Dáil, and on our way to and from class we often paused to watch the changing of the guard. In the college two large rooms had been set aside for our training course. One was the workshop where the sound of saws, planes and hammering often disturbed the quiet of the place. The other room was the drawing office where we learned draughtsmanship. The personage in charge of us was J. J. O'Connor. A large man too with a pockmarked face and a bulbous nose, he was bald with a straggling wisp which never remained plastered across his head, and stood up like an off-centre cockscomb.

He was wall-eyed, with a short upper lip from which sprung a bristly moustache. In class he was a strict disciplinarian and had a tongue so caustic it would nearly take the paint off the door. On a bad day when his temper got out of hand he hissed like a rattlesnake and could get much venom into a word like 'lout'. But on a good day his face lost its bulldog appearance and became soft and almost comic as he reminisced about the characters he knew in the trade in his native Cork. It was there J. J. and his assistant, Nicky Hartnett, started their working lives as carpenters, and fine craftsmen they were. J. J. had good stories about his apprenticeship and told of the man who when making a lavatory seat from a plain board marked the hole by drawing a line around his hard hat. He then auger-holded it, cut it out with a lock saw, and rounded it off nicely with a spokeshave.

J. J. read widely and often talked about Frank O'Connor and Sean O'Faolain, whom he said he knew. Like Mícheál Ó Riada, my teacher in Killarney, he talked to us about the theatre and was stone mad on Shakespeare. When a backward student mutilated a job of work, J. J., taking the damaged exercise, would intone:

> O, pardon me thou bleeding piece of earth,
> That I am meek and gentle with these butchers.
> Thou art the ruins of the noblest man
> That ever lived in the tide of times . . .

and standing back from the bench, and in the best tradition of a Father O'Flynn loft player, he would continue Mark Anthony's speech, and when he came to view the wounds on Caesar's body:

> Which like dumb mouths do ope their ruby lips
> To beg the voice and utterance of my tongue.
> A curse shall light upon the limbs of men;
> Domestic fury and fierce civil strife
> Shall cumber all the parts of Italy . . .

he would raise his voice to such a terrifying climax that passing professors would open the door and look in to see if all was well.

One day he made a collection and put in some money himself. I was dispatched down to Fred Hanna's to get twenty-one copies of *The Merchant of Venice*, which cost sixpence each and were in the Penguin series. Woodworking came to a halt and in the midst of wood-shavings, sawdust and chips we settled down to read the *Merchant*. I remember reading the part of the elder Gobbo, while two refined Corkmen were cast as Portia and Nerissa. Portia describing one of her suitors says: ' . . . he doth nothing, but talk about his horse, he can shoe him himself. I am much afeared, my lady, his mother played false with a smith.'

The reader made a bad fist of the speech. What he read was 'I am much afeared me mother played false with a smith.'

'Judging from the way you are stuttering over the text I don't doubt but she played false with a forge full of smiths!' J. J. said.

When the mood moved him, whatever work we were engaged in, J. J. got us to read Shakespeare. He fancied himself as an actor and often, as one of the lads used to say, he gave us a 'blaist' of Falstaff. Of course reciting Shakespeare was a useful exercise for young men who would yet have to stand before a class. To improve the voice he also got us to sing. In the storeroom where our stock of timber was kept he installed a piano; we paid the rent. One of the students was a good pianist and once a week J. J. herded us in there to sing sea shanties. He sang shantyman himself in as deep and salty a voice as ever came from a man of the sea. We joined in the chorus.

J. J.:	King Louis was the King of France
	Before the Revolution.
Students:	Away! Haul away! Haul away, Joe!
J. J.:	King Louis had his head cut off,
	Which spoiled his constitution!
Students:	Away! Haul away! Haul away, Joe!

Each student in his turn became shantyman and we sang such songs as 'Blow the Man Down', 'In Amsterdam There Lived a Maid', 'Johnny Come Down to High-lo' and 'What Shall We Do with the Drunken Sailor', which had the chorus of:

> Put him in the long boat till he's sober,
> Ear-ly in the morning.

Out of the classroom J. J. dropped his stern attitude and one night a student met him in a pub in the company of a professor from St Patrick's Training College in Drumcondra. The professor was a fellow Corkman and they both came back to our digs. They were well in their cups and sang 'The Banks' and a snatch of:

> The stench at Patrick's Bridge is wicked,
> How does Father Matthew stick it?
> Here's up 'em all, says the boys of Fair Hill!

J. J. played the cello. He gave us a short recital once in the storeroom after a sea shanty session. His assistant Nicky Hartnett played on a violin he had made himself. With the sound of music and song one day and hammering and sawing the next, we livened up the quiet atmosphere of the College of Art.

When the Free State government made Irish obligatory for technical school teachers, J. J. was sent to the Ballingeary gaeltacht in west Cork to learn the language. A teacher accustomed to standing in front of a class finds it difficult to sit in one. The recitation of the Irish tenses bored J. J. and at the break he took his cello to a neighbouring meadow, and with his back to a haycock played a lugubrious tune much to the amusement of the cattle in the next field. Gradually they stopped their grazing and in ones and twos drifted towards the fence, where they stood enjoying the music to the accompaniment of much tail-wagging.

J. J. claimed that the Irish he learned on these visits stood him in good stead afterwards. A man called Lang came from Austria to teach woodcarving at the College of Art. He and J. J. became firm friends. Lang used to take part in the famous passion play at Oberammergau, which was performed periodically by the villagers in thanksgiving for being saved from the black plague of 1633. I think he played the role of Christ. He invited J. J. to Austria one year and J. J. was never done telling us about it. Because J. J. spoke English, the local people took him to be British, which offended him very much, and when he was asked to sing at a party, to put some sort of seal on his identity he decided he'd sing in Irish. But he knew no song in the language, so what he did was to put together all the phrases he had learned in Ballingeary and sing them to the air of 'An Droimeann Donn Dílis':

Tá an cat ar an urlár
Tá sé fliuch, fan go fóill . . .

(The cat is on the floor. It is wet, wait a while . . .)

'An Droimeann Donn Dílis' is a haunting air and, being a good singer, J. J. brought down the house. The trouble was when he was asked to repeat the song he had difficulty in getting the Irish phrases in the same sequence.

We trainee teachers serving our new apprenticeship didn't mix very much with the art students of the college, but we did go to their professors for special subjects. The Dutchman, Mr Romein, was one and we also went to Mr Golden who taught freehand and object drawing. I remember for our first lesson he arranged a number of two-and-a-half-foot cubes in a certain order in the middle of the floor and added his overcoat, soft hat and walking cane. Bit by bit we got over our initial tinkering and learned to use quick confident strokes to complete the picture. To be able to sketch freely on blackboard or on paper is an important asset for a craft teacher.

A man came in to teach us Irish and another to take us for maths, but the person we looked forward to most was an instructor from Bolton Street Technical School, who had been a cabinetmaker in James Hicks's famous workshop in Pembroke Street. I have never forgotten the thrill of watching this man, Tom Mitchell was his name, make a mahogany drawer for a writing bureau. The precision with which he cut and fitted the dovetails was worthy of a watchmaker, the eye, brain and skilled fingers working in unison. He talked as he plied the dovetail saw, and related that James Hicks once had a commission to fashion a doll's house for the King of Sweden's daughter. When making the miniature furniture for the interior Hicks flattened a packing needle and sharpened it to cut the tiny dovetails for the drawers of the dressing table.

J. J. knew Hicks very well and, one time when the old man was ill, he went to see him only to find the patient sitting up in bed, a piece of mahogany between his knees, while with a spokeshave he fashioned a cabriole leg. The shavings curled from the spokeshave and spilled from the quilt on to the floor. In the midst of this highly inflammable material Hicks chain-smoked, the cigarette always in his mouth, and when he threw the spent butt into the grate the nicotine from constant smoking had turned the centre of his moustache to amber. J. J. had the same reverence for a craftsman as the Pope would have for a saint, and he took great pleasure in telling us that examples of Hicks's work were in the National Museum.

Because of his arresting appearance J. J. didn't escape the

eye of the artist, and Seán O'Sullivan painted his portrait as
J. J. posed in a *súgán* armchair he had designed and made
himself. The picture used to hang in the Crawford School of
Art in Cork, and very impressive he looked, warts and all.
Remembering the conversations he had with the artist as he
sat for his portrait, J. J. told us that Seán O'Sullivan was one
day walking through Stephen's Green. He was carrying a
portable easel and a drawing pad. Suddenly he saw a scene
he wished to capture. He hastily set up the easel, put on the
drawing pad, and in a fury of creativity his hat blew off and
sat upturned at his feet. As his pencil flew over the paper he
was too engrossed to retrieve the hat. A gentleman in spats
and morning dress paused and, seeing the upturned hat like
a begging bowl, said, 'You ought to be ashamed of yourself!
An able-bodied man like you should be working!'

J. J. claimed that Dublin was awash with philistines, and
so as to rescue us from that sad state he constantly guided
our reading and sent us to good films and to the theatre. He
said he didn't want us to be the intellectual inferiors of BAs
and BComms in our after-years of teaching in vocational
schools. He made us aware of what was going on in the visual
arts, and we had a private viewing of the Royal Hibernian
Academy exhibition which was held annually in the college.
He shepherded us upstairs to the exhibition hall before
varnishing day. Having had a training in draughtsmanship and
the application of colour, we had a fair appreciation of the
pictures. We were often the first to see the paintings that Seán
Keating and Maurice McGonigal brought out of Connemara.

To sharpen our wits J. J. encouraged debate, and warned
us against wilting alone and going to seed on a diet of fried
bread in a dull digs. My lodgings were in Adelaide Road, and
with me were two students from Cork, one from Kerry and
two from the west of Ireland. Willie Gannon, a Dublin

student, left his parents' house in the suburbs and joined us. The Adelaide Road address had once been the residence of Dr Douglas Hyde and sometimes circulars in his name sat on the hall table. The rooms were huge. There were three single beds in my room, and it was still large enough for a table in the centre where the two sharing with me and myself could study. Around it we learned to play a hand of bridge. The landlady, Mrs Harrison, had over a dozen lodgers under her care. They were all students except for one civil servant who occupied a single room at the top of the building. He came out on the landing every morning and shouted down the well of the stairs to the maid in the kitchen, 'Annie, I'll have tea, lightly browned toast and a boiled egg, please!'

As a digs it would have measured up to J. J.'s ideal of what a student's lodgings should be. After we got to know the young men from the university, arguments often raged into the small hours, and those of us from rural parts had our horizons broadened in matters of sex, socialism and almost every aspect of human activity. At night in the sitting-room when it came to us trainee teachers versus the university students, Willie Gannon was our star turn. He had read widely and knew something about everything. One medic admitted that Gannon's knowledge of medicine would get him through the first-year paper on the subject. He rattled off the parts of the body with the fluency of an Order of Malta first-aid man. At the slightest hint of indelicacy in Gannon's enumeration the two female students who made up our company betook themselves to bed. Later when voices were raised in the heat of debate, Ma Harrison would knock at the door and politely ask if we intended keeping everybody awake.

We affectionately called her 'Ma' but not to her face. She was like a mother to us and the only time she lost her temper was when some lout threw his empty cigarette packet into the lavatory bowl and blocked the system. We had a chronic medical student – he must have been thirty – and when he and his family went broke, it was said that Ma paid his fees and kept him gratis in the hope that he would pay her back when he qualified. He was still there when we left two years later. We thought that her love for him was a little more than motherly – she was still a young woman – because he spent much of his time in the family sections of the digs.

Mrs Harrison had a ramshackle country house in Shanganagh and any six who volunteered were welcome to spend the weekend there. When she knew who was going she bundled their bedclothes and night attire into the back seat of her old saloon car. One Saturday when I was walking down Merrion Square to get the Bray bus, Ma flew past with one leg of my pyjamas dangling out the side window. Because of the shortage of staff at Shanganagh we all helped in the kitchen under the direction of the senior medic who was always there. Once he accompanied us to the pub and, despite our country curiosity in such matters, he revealed nothing of his family background.

The open spaces around the house, the trees and the Wicklow Mountains to the south reminded me of home. With the busy routine at the college and the liveliness of the company in Adelaide Road, it was only now that I reflected on the life in Kerry which I had left so recently. I longed for the peace and even tenor of that time when life seemed to take its tempo from the slow gait of the cow chewing her cud as she walked home to be milked. I had the image too of the stonemason unhurriedly going to the heap of rubble, selecting a stone, eyeing it and dressing it, almost caressing it, with the hammer, before he placed it on the wall where it would sit in memory of him long after he had taken his rest in Killaha churchyard. That leisurely rhythm changed only when the sluggish stream grew to a torrent in a thunderstorm, or in the dance house on Sunday night when the music accelerated into the mad swing of the hornpipe. Then with a pang of regret I realised that that was all in the past — and a good job too maybe. Still, as I sleepily turned in my bed in Shanganagh and sagged into the foetal posture of slumber, I longed again for the times that were gone. I missed the company of the people I knew then, I missed the certainty of everything, I missed my family, and above all I missed my father and mother. At twenty-three I was too old for tears, but they weren't far away as I escaped into the land of nod.

There I was happy again on my way to school or working as a young apprentice in my father's workshop. Different aspects of my youthful past occupied my sleeping hours: the rounds on the pattern day, or walking in the inch by the *glaishe* with my love Jude on a Sunday evening fair. In time, back in Adelaide Road, my new lifestyle took over. When I slept, I stood in my dreams as a shantyman in the storeroom singing 'Johnny Come Down to High-lo' or 'Oh, You New York Girls, Can't You Dance the Polka?'

Of the twenty young men on our course all had started their working lives as carpenters or cabinetmakers. The skill in using tools they had acquired over five or six years at the bench was indispensable to their work as manual instructors. Practical experience in the handling of sharp tools was essential when it came to teaching young boys how to use these implements. Some of the men on the course had had a secondary education, but others like myself had left school at fourteen and depended on night classes at the tech to get to a standard sufficient to pass the scholarship examination. Those with a post-primary education liked to lord it over us, displaying their knowledge of Latin and Greek and quoting widely from Milton and Eoghan Ruadh Ó Súilleabháin. But we who left school early were longer at the bench and that training was what mattered in the job ahead.

As well as the subjects of Woodwork, Drawing and Maths, we were expected to have a good knowledge of Irish. To improve that knowledge, at the end of our first year, we were sent for two months to the gaeltacht of Carraroe in Galway. Two or three students stayed in each house and with our basic Irish, very basic in some cases, we managed to carry on the essential conversation of making our needs known. The local people had years of experience in dealing with the *lá breás*, as learners of the language were called. The phrase *lá breá* (fine day) was as much Irish as beginners could muster when they met a native speaker on the road. The family, as was expected of them, spoke only Irish to their visitors and went to a lot of trouble explaining words and phrases.

Two pounds ten shillings was our weekly scholarship allowance in Dublin, which was reduced to two pounds in Carraroe. The Department of Education believed it was cheaper to live in the country. A guinea went for our board and lodgings and the rest was ours to spend. The woman of the house washed our shirts, socks and underwear. Most young men smoked and a few of us drank the occasional pint, which if I remember cost eight old pence. We managed, and were able to afford to go on the odd outing.

One Sunday we went by hooker to the Aran Islands, Inis Mór to be exact. The hooker, a fishing vessel, was often used to bring turf to the islands. It was my first time in a boat as big as this, and it took a while before I got my sailor legs. We docked at Kilronan and set out on the long walk to Dún Aengus but were driven back by the rain. We took shelter in a public house, where most of the day was spent. A storm blew up and we thought we'd have to spend the night on the island. But the men in charge of the boat, having spent the day drinking, knew no fear and decided to set out for the mainland.

We were nervous enough going on board and those who enjoyed the trip standing on the deck coming over now crowded into the hold. There wasn't room for everyone and I and many more remained on deck. It was plain sailing until we got out of the shelter of the island, then the sea rose mountainous high. The ship bounced on the brine like a cork, and when it was carried high on a mounting wave we could see a great valley of water below. We held on to anything we could grasp while the waves washed across the deck. As the ship swayed, Barbara McDonagh, a young teacher from the college, stood with her back to the mast, her arms enfolding it behind her. As she sang her dark hair streamed in the storm. The inland women screamed in the hold and huddled together as they prayed to God to bring them safely home. Barbara's summer dress clung to the outline of her body as each successive wave washed over her. She was one with the mast as if sculpted, like a mascot on the prow of a viking longboat. Water spilled into the neck of my open shirt and ran down my body and into my shoes.

The skipper, showing his drink, shouted and argued with the men at the tiller, disputing which way the ship should go. In the gathering gloom there was a mighty shout. '*Na carrigreacha! Na carrigreacha!*' ('The rocks!'). The ship swerved and we could make out the sharp ridge of rock now visible, now covered by the surging sea. The wreck of the *Hesperus* came to mind, 'impaled on the horns of an angry bull!' Soon we saw the dark mass of land at both sides which meant we were in the bay leading to the pier. Gradually the water calmed and the frightened people emerged from the hold as we docked safely in the little harbour of Calladh

Thaidhg. Those of us who had stayed on deck were drowned wet. The clothes stuck to our bodies as we walked the distance to our lodgings. My wardrobe was not very extensive but I was lucky enough to have a change of trousers, a dry shirt and a pullover. The sea air whetted our appetites and we were ravenous for our supper. Afterwards we set out for the Sunday night *céilí* in the college. With the help of an Irish dancing teacher we were already able to make a fair fist of 'The Walls of Limerick', 'The Siege of Ennis' and 'The Haymaker's Jig'. The dance steps came easy to me as I had plenty of practice at set dancing at home in Kerry.

Local girls as well as visitors came to the *céilí*, and Barbara, she of the mast, advised us to dance with the local girls. We'd be killing two birds with the same stone, she claimed — improving our dancing and perfecting our Irish. I asked Barbara what I should say to my partner if I felt like seeing her home. She told me. After a few dances I met up with a young lady who was warm, friendly and attractive. When 'The Siege of Ennis' was over and the 'Soldier's Song' played, marking the end of the night, I summoned up enough courage to ask my partner, '*Bhuil tú a' dul ann?*' (Literally, 'Are you going there?') She drew herself up to her full height and said with what I thought was more than a modicum of disdain, '*Bhí mé ann cheana!*' ('I was there already!'), and flounced off.

It happened one time that we organised a *céilí* in the house where we stayed. The local people danced the Connemara set, where at the end of a figure all the dancers grasped each other around the waist and went into a wild spin, chasing the mad, galloping music until, exhausted, they came to a halt. In the pause after the dance a man came from the shadows, and with his eyes closed sang in the old way. His neighbours listened intently, their eyes fixed on the fire, the dresser, or on some object like the lamp, as the rise and fall of his voice searched out the nooks and crannies of the room. The soft words clothed in sweet melody flowed from the singer's mouth to a humming accompaniment through his nose. It was lonely, eerie and enchanting. It was the cry of a young lover poisoned by a meal prepared by his sweetheart. The song was a conversation between him and his mother:

Cad a bhí agat dod dhinnéar a bhuachaillín Ó?
Sicín go raibh nimh ann a mhaithirín Ó,
Ó cóirigh mo leapaidh, tá mé breoite go leor.

What had you for your dinner my own darling boy?
A poisonous chicken. Oh, dress my bed soon,
I've a pain in my heart and I want to lie down.

An elderly man was called upon to dance. It was easy to see that as a performer he was held in high esteem.

'What way will I give it to you?' was the accordion player's tentative question in Irish.

'Give it to me now,' the dancer said, 'according to the way you think I'll want it!'

He took his place on the flagstone in front of the fire facing the crowd. He waited with the toe of his right shoe resting on the floor. When the music struck up he sprang into action. Well, sprang is the wrong word, because unlike the stepdancers of my native place, his feet were hardly ever raised more than a few inches above the flag. He made an intricate movement with his feet using heel and toe and dancing out to fill the floor space available to him. Now and again he gave an involuntary little hop which brought a reaction from the crowd.

In one of these departures from the routine of the dance there was a commotion in the room off the kitchen. As voices were raised and as people turned in their direction, the dancer came to a halt and the music trailed away. In time we found out the reason for the disturbance. It seemed that visitors had brought a bottle of illicit spirits into the house. The abuse of *poitín* had been so bad in that district that the clergy encouraged families to have their houses consecrated to the Sacred Heart, at which ceremony a vow was made that *poitín* would never enter the homestead.

The woman of the house was devastated that the family should have broken its vow to the Redeemer. She cried openly, her lament having many echoes of the *sean nós* song we had heard a short time before. When the people responsible for bringing in the drink had been ejected, neighbours explained to her that the pledge had not been broken by a member of her family but by strangers over whom she had no control. She calmed down and after a while the *céilí* was resumed, but the spirit had gone out of the night and the family was glad when the affair was over.

Poitín-making, despite the efforts of the police to bring the illicit distillers to justice, was widespread in Connemara. Church and state were opposed to it and when the mission came every five years the Redemptorist priests preached on the evils of *poitín*. Father Conneely in the course of one of of his sermons asked the sergeant – a dark, swarthy Kerryman with a pair of enormous eyebrows that would nearly fence cows out of cabbage – to sit outside the altar-rails. The priest praised the sergeant's efforts to quell the evil practice, and likened his work to a crusade. And indicating the sergeant he said, *'Breathnaigí air, nach naomh é!'* ('Look at him, isn't he a saint!') Two old ladies in the congregation did as the priest bade them. Then one said to the other, *'Ní fheadar mé. Tá cuma a' diabhail air!'* ('I doubt it. He looks like the devil!').

Father Conneely was a thundering great preacher, a native speaker who could reduce his congregation to tears or fill their hearts with terror. He pleaded with the *poitín*-makers to bring their stills to the chapel yard. At first there was no response, but then a man giving in to the pleadings of his wife came in the darkness and placed his still by the chapel wall. Egged on by this headline and promises of glory in heaven or everlasting torture in the flames of hell, a few more stills arrived, until by the end of the week there was a great mound of corkscrew pipes in the chapel yard. Sunday night was the closing night of the mission. With lighted candles the faithful renounced the devil and all his works and pomps. Father Conneely led them out into the yard. The great heap of metal had been drenched with petrol. With a prayer he threw his lighting candle into the heap. There was a sudden blaze that reached as high as the eaves and was reflected in the church windows, giving them the quality of stained glass. The corkscrew pipes glowed red in the blaze and from the scum of alcohol secreted in the tubes a black pall of smoke with a blue-purplish flame at the centre rose to the sky. It was a dramatic moment. As the people gazed at the psychedelic design in the midst of the smoke, the priest, his arms upraised, shouted, *'Breathnaigí, a phobail Dé! Tá an diabhal ag eirí as!'* ('Behold, brethren! The devil is rising from it!')

2

A Change of Name and a Job

We left Carraroe on a bright September morning. It was 1939 and coming through Galway city we heard that Hitler's army had invaded Poland. Having learned about Pádraic Ó Conaire, the writer, in the Irish classes in Carraroe, we set out to see his statue. We found him in Eyre Square sitting with his hat on in the attitude of a *seanchaí* telling a story. I thought it a pity the sculptor hadn't depicted his *asal beag dubh* (small black donkey) standing beside him. Padraic was happy looking, forever sitting there, and the war wouldn't worry him. Nor did it worry us. We went and drank a few pints to kill the time before the train left. The crowd of us almost filled the small pub, and much to the amusement of the local clients we sang the songs we had learned in Carraroe. '*Maístir bád mór ag dhul ród na Gaillimhe*' ('Skipper of the big boat on the road to Galway') and many others like '*Bíonn caipín bán ar amadán, 's púicín ar mo ghrá*' ('A fool wears a white cap and there's a mask on my lover's face').

It took some time for the signs of war to appear in Dublin but the dark blue shades I mentioned earlier were fitted to the windows of the College of Art. Wide cowls were put over the streetlamps to keep the light on the roadway and out of the sky. It would be a while yet before food and clothes rationing was introduced. One more year was all we had to go before we qualified. That year we worked hard. We cut down on the number of times we went dancing to the Teachers' Club in Parnell Square or to Barry's Hotel. No more fly-by-night relationships with young civil servants in their first year up from the country.

The extra attention we gave to our work paid off and everybody got through the final exams. Some weeks before that testing time an advertisement for a vacancy for the post of woodwork teacher in Kerry appeared in the papers. I applied for it and I was advised by Paddy Mawe, a Corkman, that as County Kerry had two gaeltachts I should make my application in Irish. This I did and got the post. I found out later that the head man in the Kerry Vocational Committee hadn't a word of that tongue. He used to wait until an Irish teacher called to the office to translate any correspondence in the old language. He, the Chief Executive Officer, wrote back to me in English to say that I had been appointed, but when he came to my name Éamon Ó Ceallaigh he half translated it to Éamon Kelly. I was so happy to get the job that I let things rest so and the name Edmund which I had received in baptism became a part of my past life and my new name Éamon Kelly was emblazoned in the records of the Kerry Vocational Committee and in the Department of Education in Dublin.

My first job in Kerry was that of an itinerant teacher, giving a course of six weeks in woodwork in a village and then moving on. Posters with my new name writ large appeared in shop windows and in advertisements in local papers, so that everyone called me Éamon when they got over the 'Mr' stage. In time I got used to it. Ardfert outside Tralee was my first stop, and I stayed in the lodgings of Mrs O'Leary. The

hall where the classes were to be held was a short distance
away beside the ruins of the ancient cathedral. My first night
was given over to the enrolment of the students and their
introduction to the woodworking implements. I talked about
what was involved in the course and gave a lesson in planing,
sawing and chiselling. I found a place to crack a few jokes
with them as there is nothing like laughter to break the
barrier between strangers.

The next day I put a drawing of the first lesson on the
blackboard, sharpened the tools and had the wood ready on
which each student was to work. It being my first time going
before a class, I was determined that everything should be
right and of course very anxious to make a good impression.
The class was at 7.30. I left the caretaker to open the hall and
I made my entrance at the exact time to find the men, young
and not so young, all assembled. I walked up the aisle
between the workbenches with a 'good-night' left and right
and went straight to the blackboard to begin the preliminary
talk.

I was a little nervous as I removed my overcoat. I put it
on a hook and when I turned to survey the class with all the
assurance I could muster, I was greeted with a burst of
laughter. My confidence received something of a dent. I
couldn't imagine the cause of their hilarity until I noticed a
ladies' silk stocking draped over my shoulder. I managed a
weak smile and then a fit of laughter to cover my confusion.
Slowly I removed the stocking and, as I folded it, I painted
for the class a picture of Mrs O'Leary's kitchen, with a
shoulder-high clothesline between the fire and the front
door. I demonstrated to them how easy it was for the
stocking to fall on my jacket as I went to put on my overcoat.

'A good story!' one man said, while Brendan Scannell NT
took the harm out of it by saying, 'It could happen a bishop.'

I rocked on the rails but in an instant steadied myself and, with confidence restored, my first teaching lesson was a great success. There was a feeling of a bond of friendship being forged between teacher and pupils by the sharing of an unexpected experience.

Our first two weeks were spent acquiring the skill of using the carpenters' tools, and the last four in making an article of furniture of the student's own choice. Small tables were made, a *súgán* chair, presses and a meat safe. One student made, as a surprise for a devout wife, a miniature portico of a Grecian temple with a tympanum supported by four Doric pillars to hold a statue of the Sacred Heart. It had steps going up and a platform in front to hold the small red lamp. In complete contrast another student made a harrow to break up the earth of a ploughed field. The class consisted mostly of farmers and farmers' sons, with a few shopkeepers from the village and the schoolteacher, Brendan Scannell. Rich pastures and fertile tillage acres abound in North Kerry and Brendan reminded me of a verse from a poem in Irish which ran:

> *Tá an talamh comh maith san*
> *As so go Cillmhaoile,*
> *Go bhfásfadh garsún ann*
> *Comh fada le stípil!*

(The land is that good
From here to Killmoyley
That a young lad would grow there
As tall as a steeple!)

I had a junior class for boys of fourteen-plus each day, Monday to Friday at four o'clock. I taught them freehand and mechanical drawing and they learned to do woodwork exercises from drawings they had prepared beforehand. By the end of the course each student was able to take home a small medicine chest, a cutlery tray, book-ends, a toy wheelbarrow or a wall bracket to hold a Sacred Heart lamp. I had the weekends off and after a few pay cheques I bought myself a bicycle and cycled all the way to Killarney to see my parents. There was great excitement at home now. At Christmas time my brother Tim would be ordained a priest in Moyne Park, Tuam, County Galway. He had spent the years of his novitiate at Gerdingen-Bree in Belgium, and he would have been ordained in the summer, but he contracted tuberculosis and had to spend six months in a sanatorium. That he survived this dreadful disease pleased us all, but my mother more than anybody.

The ruined cathedral was near my lodgings in Ardfert and for anyone interested in craftwork there was much to be seen in the cut-stone window jambs and arches. The west doorway was Hiberno-Romanesque and in its heyday had beautiful carvings, but because they had been executed in red porous sandstone the weather of the centuries had softened and almost obliterated their definition. Around the ruin, and even within the walls, there was a graveyard with a few enormous tombs.

As they worked in class the men talked about a landlord's tomb being desecrated by vandals in search of valuables buried with the dead. In olden times, they told me, a round tower stood sentinel beside the ruined church. Because soil had been drawn away from one side of it, the tower was blown down the night of the big wind, and tradition has it that it was so well built it remained on the ground in one piece like a fallen tree trunk. They said the round tower was broken up and the stones used to build the curved entrance into Crosbie's, the landlord's place. I picked up a lot of lore in Ardfert, made many friends and downed a few pints in Flaherty's public house.

D. W. Quinlan, the chief executive officer, paid me a surprise visit in class one night and said that my next course would be in Causeway. 'You'll be in the courthouse, Mr Kelly,' he said. I had visions of an imposing Grecian-type building with Ionic or at least Doric columns supporting a sculpture-filled tympanum. When I got there I found that the court-house was a large room in a house, a one-time parlour off the grocery shop. The space was bare except for a few chairs, a rostrum and posts set into the floor with a rail on three sides to form a witness stand. With the help of the men who brought my equipment in the lorry, I had the furniture moved out to make room for the workbenches and the tool racks. With the blackboard in place I was ready for business that evening.

The course proved as popular as it had been in Ardfert. I had a full complement of boys over fourteen in the after-noon, and every bench was occupied by adults for the night class. The room wasn't very well lit and when we got down to serious work, one student brought with him a small pocket torch, which he shone on the dovetail markings with his left hand while he sawed with his right. There were many faces at the street window at night looking in. I also had an audience at the other side where there was a cow byre. Contented cows chewed the cud as their large eyes caught the light from the paraffin lamps.

When we got over the early training stage and each man was working on the project he would bring home to show his wife or his mother, many students sang as they worked, such was their enjoyment and total immersion in their new pursuit. The snatch of a love song or a whistled jig sounded pleasant over the sound of hammer and saw or the banshee wail of a pine board under a sharp plane.

I lodged in the same house and my bedroom was directly over the courthouse. As always, I found it difficult to sleep the first night in a strange bed. I was twisting and turning, dropping off and dreaming and waking up with a start. I read for a while, and before quenching the light, instead of counting sheep I counted the religious objects in the bedroom. I had never seen so many in one place except maybe in a huckster's stall at a mission. There were pictures of all shapes and sizes, statues large and small, a crucifix, a rosary, a scapular on a nail and a little glass cylinder with liquid around the figure of the Virgin. When I shook it before going to bed it filled with snow.

One picture had just the crown of thorns with globules of blood dripping from it. In the normal course of events I probably wouldn't have given the image a second thought, but now longing for elusive sleep I found the crown of thorns without the Sacred Head discomfiting. A terrifying instrument of torture, and all that blood! Blood too on the Sacred Heart, both the statue and the picture, and on the crucifix where the lance had speared His side and the nails had pierced His hands and feet. There were plenty of religious objects in my own home and in the houses in which I worked with my father, but not until tonight did something which I had always accepted become disturbing. The eyes of the pictures became riveted on me, or so it seemed, and to avoid their accusing stare I put out the light.

In time I fell into a troubled sleep. I have a knack of recalling bad dreams and that night I dreamt of ancient druids slaughtering animals and offering them as sacrifice on a stone altar that looked like a Mass rock. The celebrant, as gaunt as El Greco's St Francis, raised his eyes to heaven while the congregation in biblical-type dress beat their breasts and lifted their arms in prayerful supplication. Ferocious acolytes pounced on me and dragged me body and bones towards the altar as my clothes were stripped from my back. A knife was poised over my throat and as it came down I bawled like hell and when I woke I was sitting bolt upright in the bed with sweat streaming down my face.

There was a loud knock on the door. It was the landlady. 'It's half past ten,' she said. 'Are you all right?' 'I am,' I replied. 'I'll be down in a minute.' She must have heard me shout. Goodness knows what she thought of me. I lay on for a little while thinking of the strange dream I had, and looking at the religious objects which I assumed caused it. I thought I heard murmuring in the room below me punctuated by an occasional cough. I dressed quickly and went downstairs. I looked into my classroom of the night before to find the district court in session.

Some of the workbenches were stacked at one end of the room and some were put out in the street. The closed tool racks by the wall acted as seating for the small crowd. A half-dozen uniformed gardai stood in front of the rostrum where the district justice sat. One guard was giving evidence of catching people in a public house after hours. He claimed that when he entered the premises the bar was clear, but he found a number of men in the back yard drinking. He went upstairs to the bedroom and when he opened a wardrobe a man who had been leaning against the door fell out. In the bed two more men were sleeping. He looked closely and their eyelids fluttered a bit. They had the blankets pulled up to their chins and their feet were sticking out at the bottom.

'Did they not feel the cold?' the justice said, enjoying the scene.

'How could they, your worship,' the guard said, 'when

they had their boots on!'

The landlady tapped me on the shoulder. 'Your break-fast'll be going cold,' she said.

I followed her into the kitchen and never found out how the men and the publican fared in the justice's judgement. A fine is all he could put on the men but the publican could end up with an endorsement on his licence.

3

A Spell in Ballybunion

I spent a whole year on the road and visited all the villages of north and mid-Kerry. Often when the lorry with the equipment drew up in front of the parochial hall, youngsters would gather around chanting, 'The play actors are here again!' But when they saw the blackboard being unloaded they changed their tune to 'Come on away, lads, 'tis only an ol' school he's starting!'

In Ballybunion my classes were held in the large dining-room of Beasley's lodging house opposite the garda barracks. It was springtime and the holidaymakers hadn't yet come. Wielders of the knife and fork in that dining-room in the high season never enjoyed themselves as much as did the wielders of the chisel and saw in my class.

It is heart-warming the avidity with which men take to carpentry. There is a longing in all of us to make, to create. The way they admired the revealed grain when a sawn board was planed. They would take it up and smell the lath that came from the jack plane and fondly crush the shavings in their hands. The countryside around Ballybunion is bare of trees and the students fell in love with the different timbers they met with in the course of their work. When we talked of sycamore, ash, elm or oak, I showed them illustrations of the trees from which the wood came, or drew the oak leaf and acorn on the board, a small seedling carrying in its womb a baby king.

We remembered talk of ancient times when trees grew almost down to the seashore and Ireland was a great woodland, where squirrels could travel from Antrim to Cork without touching the ground. I cited the poet's lament for the fallen forest. *'Cad a dhéanfaimíd feasta gan adhmad/ Tá deireadh na gcoillte ar lár'* ('What'll we do now without timber/The last of the forests is down').

I made many friends in Ballybunion. I almost became an alcoholic in that place. When the class was over at night I went with Jackie Beasley on a pub crawl, as much for the craic, as they say now, as for the booze. After-hours drinking was part and parcel of the nightlife there, a legacy of the high season when the Irish seaside resorts were packed with roisterers. Holidaymakers were confined to Ireland because of the war. Publicans were anxious to keep the beer flowing. In one establishment if we dawdled over our pints the proprietress would admonish us with a 'Gentlemen, your conversation is interfering with your drinking!' The pubs were often raided after closing time but the guards didn't always prosecute. I remember one night Jackie Beasley and myself standing inside the window curtains until the sergeant had cleared the bar. When he left we emerged, called for another drink and resumed the argument which had been so rudely interrupted.

It was in Ballybunion I met Bill Kearney, an army sergeant in charge of training the Local Defence Force. We both stayed in Beasley's when he visited the place. His night-time course of training ended about the same time as my class, and he, Jackie Beasley and I often had a few scoops. Bill was a fine singer, his favourite being 'Santa Lucia', and you could hear a pin drop when he sang. When I followed with a Tan war ballad the assembled clientèle shouted, 'Will you shut up, or do you want to bring the guards down on top of us!' Bill enrolled me in the LDF, but because of my night classes I was excused from training. I had a feeling he put me down as being connected with intelligence! I did attend one church parade. I borrowed a uniform and fell in − the very last man in the line. After a while the drill sergeant bellowed, 'Will the second last man in the rank change step.' The order was for me, but how was I to know that a latecomer had fallen in behind me.

Jackie Beasley and I were detailed to stand guard one night over the LDF arms depot in a room in the barracks. We had only to cross the road. We took up duty at midnight and Jackie gave me a rifle. I wasn't too sure which end the bullet came out, but I sat there, the rifle between my knees, the muzzle pointing towards the ceiling. A civic guard slept in the room directly overhead. Before retiring he looked in on us, regarding me with a little suspicion and noting the direction in which the gun was pointing. He closed the door and a short time afterwards we heard movement upstairs. It turned out that he was taking the sandbags from the windows and putting them under his bed.

Ted Houlihan was the local officer commanding the LDF and his strategy in case of an invasion during the hours of darkness was to ring the church bell to call out the troops. When we were all in our cups one night in Gabrielle's hostelry, the son of a prominent citizen and a comrade in arms thought it would be a damn fine lark to ring the bell just to see how many would come out. Though our reasoning powers were sadly undermined by alcohol, Bill Kearney, Jackie Beasley and I persuaded him against taking such an action, which would bring us into conflict with the law and the Church. He seemed to agree but later that night as I was going to bed the bell rang out loud and clear. He had done it! I expected an immediate commotion with voices raised in the street. No. There was a deadly silence. Then the sound of doors opening in the house. Steps on the stairs and on the road outside. The fumes of the alcohol were rising to my brain. I had drunk too much that night. I became drowsy and lay back in the bed. Bacchus rolled me into the arms of Morpheus, who lolled me into a deep sleep where a tolling bell tore cracks in the silken fabric of the sky. Bright streaks ran down to earth as if made by fork lightning.

I was in the open space outside Riverview with Jackie Beasley and Bill Kearney. We were getting our rifles out of the armoury in the guards' barracks. Everyone was talking. Rumour had legs. Ballybunion was full of Germans. Hitler was seen drinking with Lord Haw Haw in JD's and Bridie skimming the froth off the pint with a white-handled knife. We'd meet the enemy, we bragged. We'd meet him on the beach. As we marched down the street, window sashes were thrown up and women in their chemises cheered us on to battle. Pat Crowley's band left the ballroom and played 'The Minstrel Boy', leading us on to the Castle Green.

Standing behind the ruined walls of O'Connor's stronghold we peered nervously in the direction of the strand. Blessed hour! What was this? In the moonlight we saw that there was nothing to battle against but the waves of the incoming tide. We cheered and let off a volley into the night air. From the sober element came a call for silence. A sound was heard high up in the sky. We listened, but it wasn't the Luftwaffe, just the *gabhairín rua* – the jacksnipe crying for his lost lover. The band struck up a wartime ditty, and I woke up singing:

Bless 'em all! Bless 'em all!
The long and the short and the tall.
Bless de Valera and Seán McEntee,
They gave us brown bread
And a half ounce of tea . . .

In the morning the talk of the town was the ringing of the church bell. The clergy at Mass likened it to a sacrilege, and the Local Defence people were livid at bringing part-time soldiers on to the street. If real danger ever came, what would be the use of ringing the church bell? In time the name of the campanologist got out. We in the know never opened our beaks. He himself must have boasted in his cups. But when it transpired that he was the son of a rich burgher closely affiliated to the powers that be, no word was said.

When I had courses in the nearby villages of Asdee and Lisselton I still lodged in Beasley's of Ballybunion. I was there in June when the holiday season was getting under way. Pat Crowley and his band were in residence and the strains of their music came from the ballroom a little after eight in the evenings. I perfected the old-time waltzing I had learned in the Teachers' Club in Dublin. Before each dance in the ballroom, soap flakes were scattered generously on the floor, which made us glide over it like sailing ships on a still ocean. One night I saw a svelte, lissom creature, divine and beautiful, and I summoned up enough courage to ask her to dance. She accepted my invitation and when the music struck up she moved with grace and rhythm. With my heart in my mouth and schooling myself to take care of my accent I was about to utter some pleasantry when she said, 'Isn't de floor awful skeety!' My Killarney patois wasn't entirely out of place that night.

Local people of the old school never wet themselves in

the brine except maybe to take a hot sea bath. Ted Houlihan who lived down on the brink of the tide told me over a pint one night in Mrs Scanlan's that he was only once in the sea and that was twenty-five miles away in Ballyheigue. On fine Sundays in summer, Ballybunion beaches were black with people. I was a poor swimmer but had enough courage to dash into the huge incoming waves where the legs were taken from under me and I was carried inshore and deposited on the sand. It was an exhilarating experience being rolled about in the water as the waves broke and crashed on the shore with the sound of thunder.

Ballybunion had two bathing places, the men's strand and the women's strand, and largely the sexes kept to these places from force of habit going back to the days of Victorian prudery. But the way of youth is to turn its back on the customs of the old, and now there was an outcry by the powers that be against mixed bathing. Brendan Behan on hearing of it said the next thing to be banned would be mixed dancing. The parish priest, a man of his time, paraded the beaches after last Mass on Sundays, and people on seeing him approach repaired to their respective places. One Sunday he accosted a middle-aged man and a young girl coming in from the sea. He admonished them for bathing together. The gentleman told him that he had been teaching his daughter to swim.

In Beasley's lodging house they talked of the day when a busload of visitors arrived from somewhere inland. Ignorant of local custom they trooped gaily down to the men's strand. The ladies, when they didn't see any other ladies about, drifted towards the women's beach. All but one; she sat among the men and was preparing to divest and take to the water when the PP arrived. Politely he requested her to move away. Very politely she told him that the man sitting next to her was her husband and that her place was at his side. The rules would have to be observed, she was told. Getting a little bolder, she said wasn't it a queer pass when husband and wife couldn't enjoy a day at the seaside together. Her husband, who was embarrassed at the attention the scene was attracting, collected up their belongings and said, 'Come on away, Mary, if he finds out we're sleeping together we'll be excommunicated!'

After Ballybunion and Asdee my travels brought me to Tarbert and Moyvane, where I had to call on the parish priest Father Danny O'Sullivan to get permission to use the parochial hall. The housekeeper showed me into the parlour, and in an adjoining room there were people talking. This lasted for some time and when they left Father O'Sullivan came into the parlour with a soda siphon hanging from one hand and a whiskey decanter in the other. When he saw me he swung them both behind his back, making a loud clatter. Thinking he had some damage done he turned them around quickly, examined them and put them on the sideboard.

I explained my business. The hall would be all right. He had let it to the Vocational Committee previously. I thanked him and was about to go when he eyed me up and down and said abruptly, 'Where are you from?' My parents, I told him, were born in the parish of Rathmore, but I was brought up near Killarney. That interested him. Rathmore was his native village, where his people owned the well known public house, the Southern Star. I told him a little more about my family. The men were carpenters, I said. He remembered my grandfather, Brian Kelly, and often saw him lift his elbow in the Southern Star.

'A little dram,' he continued indicating the siphon and the decanter, 'helps to drive a bargain' and he mentioned that his visitors were arranging for a wedding, part of which proceedings was deciding the amount of the marriage offering. The offering is calculated on so much per cow, he said, and fixing me with a doleful eye he sighed, 'Farmers have many cows when they want a new creamery but very few when it's money for a marriage offering!' Then he said with a smile, 'A little drop of Robin Redbreast softens their hearts and I made a good bargain.'

Having explained away the presence of the siphon and the decanter he asked another abrupt question: 'Were you in Ballybunion?' I told him I had spent a few months there. 'Well,' he said, 'the good man who was parish priest in Ballybunion when I was a young curate told me that he was once discussing a marriage offering with a farmer. Five pounds is all he could get out of the man, so he went to the sideboard and produced the bottle. After a glass of whiskey the farmer went up two pounds ten shillings. He filled the glass again and the man went up to ten pounds! The next day the parish priest was walking in the village and there was a publican standing at his door. "Tell me, John," the priest said, "how much are you getting for your whiskey?" "Ten pence a glass, Father!" the publican said. "Ah John, you are a poor salesman!" the priest laughed. "I got two pounds ten a glass for mine last night."'

There was one last question. 'Have you brothers?'

'I have,' I told him. 'Four, and one of them will be ordained at Christmas time.'

He reached for the decanter and poured a stiff one for himself and a modicum for me.

4

In the Mail Car to Waterville

Around this time a letter came from the CEO to say that my post as itinerant teacher would end at the summer holidays, and in September I would take up duty as manual instructor at the Vocational School in Waterville. The only way of getting from my home to Waterville was by mail car, in which there was room for maybe a half dozen passengers. It passed by our place at the unearthly hour of 6.30 a.m. and I would be in Waterville before the school opened on the first morning in September 1941. I was the only passenger for ages. We drove by the Robber's Den, where the Black Rogue of Glenflesk had a school for thieves. Some of these emigrated and their descendants, for all we know, could have been implicated in the St Valentine's Day Massacre in Clarke Street, Chicago. Through the Roughty Valley we went, by Kilgarvan and Kenmare and then on to Sneem where John Millington Synge's blue bull came from.

The mail car was filling up now and there wasn't really room for a party of three young girls at Lohar. The driver asked me if I'd take one of them on my knee. I did, and this made for a little hilarity among the others. She was a frolicsome damsel, very shy at first on having to sit on a strange man's lap. I was a little embarrassed myself at all the attention we were getting from the passengers, the driver saying what a fine match we'd make. 'Hold on to him, girl, maybe he has money!' She had to hold on to me because of the bumping of the car on the rough road – an altogether refreshing experience. Ballinskelligs Bay came into view and I asked her if she had ever been to the Skelligs Rock.

'She might have to go there yet,' one of her friends remarked, 'if she isn't married before Shrove Tuesday!'

The young lady was echoing the stories of her father's fireside. The monks on Skelligs Rock monastery didn't recognise the Gregorian calendar of 1582 and Shrove Tuesday fell eleven days later. People who weren't wed by the Shrove Tuesday deadline before Lent on the mainland, could go to Skelligs and be spliced on the Rock. At home when I was a youngster if people eligible for marriage hadn't taken the plunge before Lent, their names, often matched with the most unlikely candidates, were penned in rhyme and pushed under the doors of the laggards on Shrove Tuesday night. The document was called the 'Skelligs List'.

We were in Waterville and the young lady, giving me a playful 'dunt' of her elbow, eased herself and her belongings off my lap and alighted. I went to the lodging house I had booked. Muiris Mac Gearailt, the teacher of Irish and Maths, was staying there. Having made the acquaintance of mine host and his wife, I had a cup of tea with Muiris, then together we went to the school to meet the other two teachers, P. B. Breathnach, the headmaster, who taught Rural Science and English, and Maura Thompson, the Domestic Economy instructress. Maura knew J. J. O'Connor, my old teacher in the College of Art, which gave us something to talk about. I was told that the headmaster was a stickler for discipline. He had a goodly amount of white in a flashing eye which made him stern of demeanour, but he turned out to be witty and had a wicked sense of humour.

He had to work hard to keep up the numbers in a catchment area which was but a narrow inhabited corridor between sea and mountains on the road between Sneem and Cahirciveen. He and the school became known beyond the village because of a scheme he initiated to bring boarders from beyond cycling distance. The students lodged in the village from Monday to Friday and had a system of bringing their week's food supplies, which the landladies cooked for them. Making second-level technical education available to those who would otherwise have been deprived of it brought P. B. Breathnach to the notice of the press, and Keys Von Hoek, the popular columnist, visited us and devoted his entire article to the school in the much reduced wartime *Irish Independent*.

My first class on the morning I arrived was freehand drawing with the senior Domestic Science ladies. I made off my classroom and put out the drawing boards, pencils and drawing pins. As the young women were taking their places I went to the blackboard with a *'Dia's Muire dhíbh ar maidin'* ('Good morning, everyone') to write a few notes on the rules of perspective. I turned around to face the class and there in the second row was the young woman who had been sitting on my lap in the mail car.

I must have lit up like benediction for a titter went through the class. Shades of my first evening in Ardfert; but they had been men. I suddenly realised that with these young women I was in entirely different territory. I had to think of something quick. I drew a duck, comical but recognisable, on the board. There is something mildly ridiculous about a duck, and I told them that when God had finished making the animals at the creation of the world the angels asked Him

43

to make a duck. 'For goodness sake,' they said to Him, 'give us a laugh!'

'He made a duck . . . well a pair, and when they waddled away' — I did a waddle — 'the angels went into kinks of laughter,' and so did the class. I drew a rooster as if in conversation with the duck and said, 'A cock made fun of a duck and mocked him about his droll waddle and the way he is always nodding his head. "I'm as good as you any day," the duck said, "and to prove it I challenge you to a race!" "Game ball," says the cock. "But I'll have to pick the place," says the duck. "All right," says the cock, "but I'll have to pick the time." "Come on!" says the duck. "I'll race you across the river!" "OK," says the cock, "when there's ice on it!"'

The two stories worked. The students' laughter and mine restored my confidence. I was in control. I could look them in the eye, even the mail car lady, and the class went ahead in great style. I gradually got into the swing of teaching in a school as opposed to my itinerant courses, and once I had my syllabus made out for each class I grew to enjoy the work. There was a war and there were shortages but we never saw a hungry day. The newspapers, which came in late in the afternoon, were down to seven pages. In the digs a crackling radio brought stories of the fighting, and sometimes the voice of Lord Haw-Haw predicting a victory for Germany. But except for the occasional drone of planes high up in the skies, the hostilities could have been a thousand miles away.

English children were being evacuated from their homes in the big cities and some of them found their way to Ireland. In the first-year boys we had Tony Swatton from London. Tony's sallow complexion and his being in long trousers before his time marked him out from the other boys. The Irish in the language class was too advanced for a beginner. To keep him occupied he joined the first year for woodwork in my room. He had a particular flair for drawing and loved copying pictures or designs which I gave him. In the *Capuchin Annual* of the day, Richard King had illustrated Patrick Pearse's poem, '*Mise Éire*', surmounted with the stylised face of the beautiful Mother Ireland, and a design to enclose the words of the poem. Tony copied it to perfection, his lettering faultless, but where the name Padraig Mac Piarais was at the end, he penned 'Tony Swatton'. Years afterwards I was in Edinburgh and in a city art gallery. About to enter one room I noticed a group of navy ratings around a picture. They were being lectured on the finer points of the painting by able seaman Tony Swatton. I retraced my steps, glad he didn't see me but delighted to know that Tony hadn't lost his interest in art.

Practical subjects have such an appeal for students at a Vocational School that they rush into the room at the start of the class, and when the bell goes at the end they are lazy to leave. The girls loved the kitchen classroom where cookery and sewing were taught, the boys the garden where they learned about growing things and how to keep bees. They were happy too in my classroom where they worked at the bench and learned to make things with their hands. Their academic subjects were not neglected. They studied Irish, English, Maths and Civics. They did a play with Muiris Mac Gearailt for the end of term, when those who could dance danced and the musical ones sang or played the fiddle.

As well as the huge garden there was a playing field attached to the school where the boys played football. Muiris Mac Gearailt was the games master and, Waterville being on the edge of the Ballinskelligs gaeltacht, Irish was the language of the pitch. A field away the cable station was still tapping out its messages to distant shores. The 'graphers', as the operators were called, were principally English, and on a fine day they donned their whites and played cricket. In the still air you could hear cries of 'Howzat?' and 'Well held, sir!' mingling with shouts of, *'Buail é!'* ('Kick it!') and *'Téir isteach fé!'* ('Go in under it!').

Across the road from where Muiris and I lodged was the Butler Arms Hotel. On nights when we didn't have a class or at weekends we sometimes adjourned there for a drink. There was a lower bar, as it was called, opening on to the main street, where the natives were served. We went there and talked in Irish to the few who still knew the language, but as often as not we entered by the gate through the gravelled front to the upper bar within the hotel proper. The surroundings here were more luxurious and the drinks priced accordingly. Even in winter there were guests; some permanent residents included retired colonels and ex-British military men enjoying the quiet of neutral Ireland. In the daytime they fished in Lough Currane. I often saw them set out suitably dressed for the occasion, their gillies walking ten paces ahead carrying the fishing tackle. This apartheid was strictly observed until they sat in the boat. There was a tiled space by the reception desk where, in the evenings, the anglers laid out their catch in neat rows: fish with their mouths open and eyes glazed for all to see and admire. If they were left there too long the place smelled like Billingsgate.

In the winter of 1943 there was an occurrence in nearby Lohar which set the whole parish agog. A man was found dead in his cowhouse. He had passed out under a cow's head and the animal was thought to have gored him. But there was something about the wound that made the police suspicious. An autopsy showed that the victim had been shot at close range. The dead man, O'Sullivan, nicknamed *Cá Bhfuil Sé*, was married but childless and his wife's nephew,

O'Shea, lived in the house. Relations were said not to be so good between the two men. Suspicion fell on the nephew and on a friend of his called Brennan. The guards in their investigations found it very difficult to get information about the murder out of the local people. They talked Irish among themselves to confuse their questioners. It was common knowledge that one man heard a shot at a certain time on the night of the crime. The police were wise to this but left it until the end to interrogate him. When the individual was finally asked the question, 'And at what exact time did you hear the shot?' He looked at his questioner in blank amazement and said, 'Fhot shat!'

They were a tight-lipped community. A local shopkeeper, lowering the lid over his left eye, told me that a man working in a field overlooking the Cow and Calf Islands, near the Bull Rock, was asked by a guard, 'What islands are they?' 'God, I don't know,' the man said, gazing at them in astonishment, 'they weren't there at all this morning!'

During the investigations detectives and high-ranking gardai stayed in the Butler Arms Hotel. They were so long there and the food was so good that their cheeks filled out and they had to loosen their belts. On seeing these well-fed sleuths trooping out after breakfast one morning, one ex-colonel exclaimed to a friend, 'Swelling wisably!' Finally the nephew, O'Shea, was charged with the murder, as was his friend Brennan. At O'Shea's trial in Dublin a local witness giving evidence was asked by the judge to speak up. While the witness was still in the box, the lawyers put their heads together to discuss a point of law, whereupon the witness shouted, 'Speak up, I can't hear ye!'

The prosecution failed to make a case and O'Shea was acquitted. Brennan was subsequently charged with the same murder but was also found not guilty. The murder weapon was never found but as was remarked at the time, 'Who in his right mind would go looking for a gun in a church?'

How did the victim come by the name *Cá Bhfuil Sé*? It seems O'Sullivan was a blow-in from beyond Sneem. Before he left his native place he had, as they put it there, 'taken a girl off her road'. When he went back to a wake some twelve months later someone told the young lady that he was in the crowded kitchen. She rushed about excitedly shouting, '*Cá bhfuil sé? Cá bhfuil sé?*' ('Where is he?').

5

LISTOWEL

You got your wits sharpened in Listowel, where I went after a few years in Waterville. Vocal dexterity was an absolute necessity to parry the raillery of tavern or highway. It wasn't unknown to hear two men, oblivious of the crowds, taunting each other in high good humour across a busy street. There could be a sting too, if your sparring partner thought of taking you down a peg. I was often told to go back to the RMC. To the assembled populace this might be something Royal, Magnificent and Cornucopian. But no. It simply meant the Remote Mountainy Coomb where I first saw the light of day. The people of the parish of Prior in the diocese of Ardfert and Aghadoe were so knowledgeable that it was held that a week spent there was as good as a year at school. Listowel is like that. A year spent there is as good as three at a university.

It is a place of books and ballads, of drama and dance and walks by the Cows' Lawn and around Gurtinard to clear the head. It is a place where the people take a lively interest in the world and a livelier interest in his wife. Ears are forever cocked for the sound that comes on the breeze, and eyes are always peeled for the unusual happening. It is a place never to fall asleep on your feet or someone will build a nest in that unlistening ear. Listowel people love their town as the poets Aogán and Eoghan Ruadh loved Sliabh Luachra. Bryan MacMahon wrote lovingly about the place and his ballad about the Feale, the river named after a goddess, is a favourite song of singer Garry McMahon. John B. Keane describes the town as 'my native beautiful Listowel, serenaded night and day by the gentle waters of the River Feale; Listowel where life is leisurely and beauty leads the field, where first love never dies and the tall streets hide the gentle lovingness, the heartbreak and the moods, great and small of all the gentle souls of a great and good community' (*Irish Times* interview with Eileen Battersby, 4 April 1996).

It was a lucky day for me the day D. W. Quinlan, CEO, directed my footsteps there to take over the post of manual instructor in the technical school. Had I missed out on Listowel, God only knows into what forsaken rural or urban byway I would have walked. One of the first people I met there was Bryan MacMahon. Bryan had a lending library, and taking out a book I gave my name, Éamon Kelly. 'Come here,' he said, 'didn't I hear that name called out on the wireless the other night?' Well, it so happened that he did. Austin Clarke had a poetry competition on the radio and I had entered a poem describing my work as an itinerant teacher of woodwork. I didn't get a prize, but like the mongrel at the dog show, I was highly commended. That gave Bryan a handle on me.

At this time he was becoming well known as a short story writer, and I can still recall his joy on opening the slightly off-white wartime pages of *The Bell* magazine and seeing in print his prize-winning story, 'The Ring'. 'The Good Dead in the Green Hills' was another story of this time about a rambling house in Gleann a' Phúca where the last storyteller was ensconced as the radio pulled his audience away from him. We often met two doors down from his house in Dan Flavin's bookshop. We sat in Dan's kitchen and heard him recite again for us 'The Sally Ring' by Patrick Kelly. 'The only thing he wrote, blast you!'

Within the Ring o' Sallies
I'll build a house o' stone
A little house and white with lime
And thatched with sedge o' yestertime
And live me all alone
Within the Ring o' Sallies
Where I was sometime known.

Bryan's consuming interest then was the Listowel Drama Group, over which he presided and whose plays he directed. I had been on stage a few times in Waterville and my happiness knew no bounds when he invited me to join the Drama Group. Our rehearsals were in the scouts' hall in Market Street, where I made the acquaintance of the dapper Timothy 'Fitzmarshal' Cotter, who trod the boards with distinction. John Flaherty was another wonderful actor, as were Brendan Carroll and Bill Kearney whom I had met earlier in Ballybunion. Other talented people were Kevin Donovan, Mary Cronin, Marie Keane-Stack and Vera McElligott.

Our writers in residence were Bryan Michael O'Connor, which was the quill name of Bryan MacMahon, Michael Kennelly and Paddy O'Connor. They gave us material which was our own to tease out and put together on the floor. It was the perfect theatrical activity of writer and actor working hand in hand, and we had remarkable local success with titles like *Fledged and Flown* and *The Cobweb's Glory*, which last I found the confidence to direct myself. Next came Bryan

MacMahon's own play *The Bugle in the Blood*. For this production I wore three hats, those of set designer, director and actor. Tim Danaher did the lighting, and empty biscuit tins with hundred-watt bulbs inside were our footlights.

I played the part of the strongman, Circus Jack. I had to wear long sleeves so that my unmuscular arms weren't seen when I lifted a cartwheel to balance it on my chin. My memory holds one scene, kept fresh by recurrence, of this memorable play, in which Bill Kearney played the part of an Indian peddler who lodged in the house. He sat by the range in a darkened kitchen waiting for a chicken to cook. With the red glow of the fire on his sheet-draped figure he swayed a little as he sang, half to himself, a lonely Indian song. The lights in the kitchen had been lowered out of respect for the funeral of a hunger striker which would soon pass outside. Already the car lamps were making long ladders of light in the sky over Treen Hill.

When at last the measured beat of footsteps and the rhythmic purr of slow motor engines were heard in the street, the Indian's song gave way to the pipes playing 'The Flowers of the Forest'. Faintly the soul-stirring music faded in on the left of the stage monitor, rose to a climax and faded out on the right. A light reflection from each passing car lit the set for a while and then the Indian's song was heard again.

Bryan's play had a successful run at the Abbey Theatre. Along with Sigerson Clifford his name was added to that of George Fitzmaurice as playwrights representing the Kingdom. Bríd Ní Loinsigh the Kerry actress played the part of the mother and Jack McGowran sang the Indian song.

I was every day of thirty-five years when I took the part of Christy Mahon in *The Playboy of the Western World*. But I was thin and spare and a Kerry cap – Christy came from there

— covered a receding hairline. Characters in the play talked of Christy as 'a small low fellow, dark and dirty, an ugly young streeler with a murderous gob on him!', though in the love scene Pegeen Mike tells Christy that he is 'a fine handsome young fellow with a noble brow!' If nature hadn't supplied some of these attributes I could fake them. Dress might make the man! John Flaherty, a tailor in real life, made a jockey's colourful coat and knee-breeches with suitable headgear for me to wear at the races 'on the sands below'. I strutted the stage in this finery to see if I could ever give the impression of 'a young gaffer who'd capsize the stars!'

The Playboy of the Western World is nowhere without his sidekick, Pegeen Mike. Maura O'Sullivan, new to the company, and who had been described as a breath of fresh air by adjudicator Mícheál Mac Liammóir when we took *The King of Friday's Men* to the Kerry Drama Festival, was cast in the part. From the first reading she was simply glorious and went on to win the best actress award in Limerick. Maura and I threw our whole being into the playing. We gloried in Synge's beautiful language, so in keeping with the rise and fall of the lilting Kerry speech in lines like:

Pegeen: And it's that kind of a poacher's love you'd make, Christy Mahon, on the sides of Neifin, when the night is down?

Christy: It's little you'll think if my love's a poacher's or an earl's itself, when you'll feel my two hands stretched around you, and I squeezing kisses on your puckered lips, till I'd feel a kind of pity for the Lord God is all ages sitting lonesome on His golden chair.

Pegeen: That'll be right fun, Christy Mahon, and any girl would walk her heart out before she'd meet a young man was your like for eloquence, or talk at all.

Christy: Let you wait, to hear me talking, till we're astray in Erris when Good Friday's by, drinking a sup from a well, and making mighty kisses with our wetted mouths, or gaming in a gap of sunshine, with yourself stretched back to your necklace in the flowers of the earth.

Pegeen: I'd be nice so, is it?

Synge's words would coax the birds from the trees, and Pegeen's speeches wove a mesh of love to capture Christy Mahon's heart. Love that was make-believe on the stage became real in every waking hour. Marriage was proposed and with her father's blessing I married Maura in Killarney's tall cathedral. We went to live in a house in the Bridge Road in Listowel, but not for long. The *Playboy* won many awards. It was broadcast from Radio Éireann when radio was a power in the land, and if you walked down Church Street in Listowel that Sunday night Synge's gallous language came floating from every casement. Maura and I were asked to do an audition for the Radio Éireann players. This we did. We were successful and came to live in Dublin.

Before I leave that hallowed ground I must tell of a man I met who made a lasting impression on me. He was Maura's father Mícheál Ó Súilleabháin, a Maths and Irish teacher in St Michael's College. Mícheál came from a background in west Cork similar to my own, a place of rambling houses, endless talk and stories that went back to Conán Maol and the Giolla Deachair. He had grown up on a farm there during the last stages of the transition from spoken Irish to English. Like the Tailor Buckley of Gougane Barra, he knew the names in the old language of every flower, shrub and tree; every prominent rock and stream; every field and lake and the story behind them. Loch an Dá Bhó Dhéag, the Twelve-Cow Lake, was associated with *an Ghlas Ghaibhneach*, the celebrated grey cow of mythology. The field where she grazed and slept was forever more fertile. She gave an unending supply of milk for the needy, but the evil Balor stole her and sold her milk for profit. She escaped, and with her twelve daughters jumped into the Twelve-Cow Lake and left a greedy land behind her.

Mícheál carried in his head a now forgotten world. He drew me into this eldorado, where at night-time when stories were told in his father's house, *An Peacach 's an Bás* took the floor. The actor playing the part of Death took the scythe from the hedge outside and entered. The Sinner cowered on the settle, imploring the reaper to leave him for another while in this vale of tears. But Death persisted in his requisition and despite the Sinner's pleas for mercy and those of his neighbours, Death won the argument and took the Sinner into the outer darkness.

That was followed by *An Siota 's a Mháthair* where a patient mother tried to placate a gluttonous lump of a son who had her beggared providing him with food. The actors walked around the kitchen as if they were on a country road. The mother first, saying, *'Téanam ort! Téanam ort! Téanam ort!'* ('Come on! Come on! Come on!'). And he lagging behind like a snail going to Jerusalem, smelling the flowers, listening to the birds singing, picking blackberries and eating crab-apples until he was fit to burst. She threatened him that if he didn't control the hunger demon in his belly, when he died he'd roast in hell. But if he ate in moderation and fasted during Lent, he'd go to heaven where he'd live in a splendid house with flower-bedecked fields in front and back, and the air forever filled with music and the swish of angels' wings.

'Wisha, Mother,' he'd say, 'if there's nothing in heaven only angels and music what am I going to fill my belly with?'

On St Bridget's Eve the young men and women of that locality dressed in the most outlandish clothes they could find, the men often in women's attire and the young women maybe in their fathers' Sunday suits. To make recognition more difficult they masked their faces with pieces of old lace curtain and pulled their hats down over their eyes. The evening before, they had sculpted a face on a turnip, with the eyes and the mouth deeply incised and the inside of the turnip scooped out. They put a lighting candle into it. In the dark the light coming through the eyes and the mouth looked eerie. The sculpted head was fixed on a broom handle with a bar across to hold a coat, and with a headscarf and a skirt the effigy of Bridget called *an Brídeóg* was taken from house to house. When the mummers and the musicians came to the storyteller's house the floor was cleared, the music struck up and they danced *Gáirdín na Nóinín* ('The Garden of Daisies'). The *Brídeóg,* not the Christian Bridget who built the church in Kildare, but a priestess of the ancient druids, was held high and money was collected.

In the house that night you had all the rude elements of the theatre. The storyteller provided the comedy and some-times the tragedy, for he could bring a tear as well as a laugh. All the basic ingredients were there: the music, the dance and the dressing up.

Mícheál is now with all his neighbours in that eldorado in the skies, but the Irish spoken in his native Coomerkane is still to the good in his translation of A. E. W. Mason's novel, *Clementina*.

On the second day of February 1959 all heaven broke

loose in Listowel with the production of a new play, *Sive* by John B. Keane. At first people didn't know how to pronounce the word. They weren't sure if it rhymed with 'give' or 'hive'. It was of course the lovely Irish name Sadhbh, of which the diminutive is Saidhbhín, as in the town Cahirciveen. In the play the young schoolgirl, Sive of the title, is being traded off in marriage to an old toothless hill farmer. It is a tale of poverty and greed, of humour and tragedy, and has a show-stopping duo of travelling folk, Pats Bocock and his son Carthalawn — a singing and *bodhrán*-playing Greek chorus.

The play was given a splendid production by Listowel Drama Group, directed by Brendan Carroll and with new people like Nora Relihan and Hilary Neilson. It won all before it at drama festivals and, because it was an all-Ireland winner at Athlone, the group was invited by the Abbey to play for a week at the National Theatre then at the Queen's. Like the plays of Bryan MacMahon, Pauline Maguire and Sigerson Clifford, *Sive* drew crowds as Kingdom residents in the metropolis dipped into their savings and bought tickets to the theatre. If you had lost track of a Kerry relative, the Queen's in Pearse Street was a likely place to meet him that week.

Maura and I, who had come to Dublin seven years before, invited them all to our house one night after the show. Players and crew and friends filled our semi-detached in Coolock to bulging point. There was only one house of lords, and the gentlemen, considerate as ever, left that for the use of the ladies, while they, when the need arose, retired to the back lawn. They brought their conversation with them as they stood in a circle under a watery moon. In the weeks that followed, the wetted grass grew tall, lush and a shade of dark green, so that a little patch of Dublin was forever Listowel — maybe not forever, but for very many moons.

6

ON THE RADIO

When Maura and I came to Dublin to join the Radio Éireann Repertory Company in July 1952, we first stayed in an upstairs flat at Mountshannon Road in Rialto. The little kitchen where we cooked and dined overlooked the canal, and at that time boats drawn by horses on the tow-path passed by fairly often. Many is the morning, as I watched the lazy gait of the animal and the slow progress of the boat, I listened to Denis Brennan read the 9 a.m. news. It was Radio Éireann's first venture into early morning broadcasting, brought about by a newspaper strike in Dublin. The radio was all right, one Dublin lady said, but you couldn't put it around chips.

The old couple who owned the house hadn't an idea of where Maura and I worked, and when we were in a Sunday night play we rehearsed the script in the flat. Sometimes, carried away by the drama, we raised our voices, often in acrimony. We were once cast as the servant boy and the servant girl in a play, *Michaelmas Eve* by T. C. Murray. The characters had fallen in love but the servant boy through the scheming of his mother married the daughter of the house, no oil painting. Because of this the servant girl was livid, and when the pair were alone she gave full vent to her fury. Her language, often intemperate, contained threats like: 'I could choke and strangle you!' Hearing that row overhead the old couple were in trepidation, convinced that murder would soon be done under their roof!

Finding them anxiously listening on the stairs when I opened the door one night, I thought I had better explain the situation. I felt that it strained their credulity quite a bit to hear that we were actors on the wireless, and that our raised voices meant that we were practising our lines. Going to the studio that Sunday evening, I left the radio page of the Sunday paper with the play and the time of the broadcast marked on it on the hall table. When they heard the key in the door on our return that night the man and his wife were in the hall to greet us. They brought us into the sitting-room and made coffee. What they couldn't get over was that the voices they were listening to now had been on the radio a short time before. They were thrilled, they said, but I think what pleased them most was that the voices they had heard raised in anger upstairs weren't real after all.

We had two ardent fans while we were in that house. Of course they were sometimes disappointed because we didn't always have as big a part as we had in *Michaelmas Eve*. Sometimes, as in rep work, it was only a walk-on. The man of the house, after he had heard me in a few bit parts, advised me when I was next on the radio to hold my place at the microphone and not let the Dublin lads shoulder me off it!

Radio Éireann at that time occupied the attic of the General Post Office overlooking Henry Street and Moore Street. Through sound-baffled windows you could see the great mounds of oranges and cabbages in the traders' stalls below. Seagulls sat on the windowsills, and by the vigorous movements of their beaks they seemed to be protesting loudly at the content of the material being broadcast. There were two studios, one large and one not so large, with drapes sagging from the rafters and collar braces to improve the sound. Here all our work as actors was done, Sunday night and midweek plays, short stories, reading the linking scripts in music programmes, G. O. Sherrard's gardening account, and *Sports Stadium*. I figured prominently in this last, giving voice to the report from the south. Reading the Dublin report one evening, an actor not fully *au fait* with GAA clubs called the Faughs 'the Fucks', which made for no mean hilarity in the Green Room and red faces in the balance and control. The balance and control was the large glass box between the two studios, where the sound engineer, the disc-man and the producer sat to regulate all activities in the studios.

To get to these halls of merriment you entered the building at Henry Street, went up in the lift to the third floor and walked through a long corridor known as the 'Wood of the Whispering' (from a play of that name by M. J. Molloy). The administrative offices opened off each side of this passageway and heads of departments met there to discuss business. They lowered their voices as you approached in case they gave away any secrets. At the end of the corridor a narrow stairs brought you to a sort of lobby leading to the two studios.

In this space there was always a policeman on duty during broadcast hours to guard against IRA infiltration. A monitor brought him the programmes as they went out. Thomas Studley, a leading actor in the Rep, was one night reading a very funny short story. He came out of the studio afterwards to find the guard in contortions of laughter. Beating his thigh in paroxysms of merriment he said to Tom, 'In the Abbey you should be putting it over!' Other guardians of the law took their duties a little more seriously. The newscaster Tom Cox told me that he had started the 8 a.m. bulletin one morning when a young man walked into the studio, sat down and put a revolver on the desk in front of him. In the best traditions of the business, though the words were hopping off the page, Tom carried on and finished the news. Then on enquiry the young man told him he was a detective from the Special Branch sent to prevent the news being taken over by subversives. No standing outside for him. There is a saying in Irish, 'If a goat goes to church, the altar is his destination!'

Around this time, or maybe later, a very posh announcer came to Radio Éireann. The imperial timbre of his voice evoked echoes of the ascendancy calling from their carriages to the tradesmen in country towns. He was so grand that he put the cream of BBC newscasters in the shade. People protested. It was claimed that it wasn't our own radio station any more, that it wasn't redolent of its surroundings. Eventually the announcer left and became the presenter of a dry-cleaning sponsored programme. The radio director, Maurice Gorham, was asked why the man had been relieved of his post, to which he replied, 'We always send our best things to Imco!'

Rumour had it that a newsreader went to confession in the Pro-Cathedral. She had been partying the night before. She knelt in the box, and because the penitent at the other side had such a long story to tell, she fell asleep. Suddenly the shutter came across with a clatter. She woke up and said, 'Radio Éireann. Here is the news!'

A newsreader in Irish placed his hat on the desk beside the microphone as he read and when he announced the death of a prominent citizen he raised his hat as he said, 'May God have mercy on his soul!'

Around 1954 we actors left our old haunts in the attic, came down the stairs, through the Wood of the Whispering corridor, and turned the corner into new quarters facing

O'Connell Street. The people who paid 3d to go to the top of Nelson's Pillar could look in the windows at us going merrily down the passageway to the new studios. There were two, one large and one middle-sized, and several smaller cubicles for reading short stories, chat shows and disc jockey programmes. In contrast to the attic, everything was new except the floorboards, which creaked through the carpet and the sound was picked up by the large kidney-shaped microphones.

We got to know where the mighty creaks were and avoided them. Sometimes in a run-through of a play one would forget, and producer Séamus Breathnach would shout from his glass box, 'Merciful hour! Will you get off that creaking board!' When actors in high spirits indulged in a little horseplay at rehearsals, Séamus once gave vent to an expression which has gone into radio folklore: 'Will ye stop the acting and get on with the bloody play!'

Mícheál Ó hAodha was head of drama and variety in the station and also produced plays. He was the first to use the new studios. And it was from them he directed the poetic plays of Padraic Fallon. *The Vision of Mac Conglinne*, which had a Munster king with a hunger demon in his belly, I remember best. Sides of beef, legs of lamb and roasted piglets were washed down his gullet with churns of buttermilk. His queen, as odd as bedamned, swallowed a fly in a cup of whey and became pregnant. Fallon's plays were an undoubted success, his language matching the outlandish imagery of the folktale.

Mícheál produced a strange play called *The Paddy Pedlar* by M. J. Molloy. It was a one-act, meant for the stage, in which a near-demented man, the Pedlar, carried his dead mother on his shoulders in a sack, bringing her across forbidding landscapes to find her family burial place. A promise to the dead must be fulfilled. He talked to his mother in the sack and his cry of love for her was soul-searing, as was his simmering hatred for his cruel father who had brought her so much pain. In his voice the Pedlar endured again his mother's suffering as he described how his father 'fisted her down on the mouth!' The part of the Pedlar was beautifully and frighteningly played by Éamon Keane. I was Uaisle, owner of the house where the Pedlar sought shelter on his journey. Uaisle was a step above his station, a man who put his words on edge, mimicking the verbal precision of his betters.

Julia Monks, writing in the *Irish Press* on 22 November 1954, said, 'One of the most remarkable things about the production – apart from the incandescent acting of Messrs Keane and Kelly – was the fact that if ever a play was written for the stage and not for radio this was it . . . How Mr Ó hAodha worked the trick of making us see – almost smell – what was going on defeats me. For it was by no means an acting, or "effects" job alone. It was let's say, just magic – ever so slightly off white magic. Whatever happens don't miss the repeat. And turn down the lights and hold on to your seats!'

Radio drama in the days before the goggle-box took the spotlight off it!

There were over twenty actors in the Rep, falling, because of their stage experience, into what I'll call Gate and Abbey traditions. We had our Lady Bracknells and our Queen Gertrudes, our Bessie Burgesses and Widow Quins, our Ophelias and Pegeen Mikes. We had too our Joxer Dalys and our Old Mahons, our Mark Anthonys and Brutuses, our White-Headed Boys and our Playboys of the Western World. We were virtually an All-Ireland side, with actors from the city and from the regions, so that drama of town and country was presented with a deal of authenticity.

Two actresses did their work in Irish and English, Maura O'Sullivan and Neasa Ní Annracháin. Eight actors appeared in plays and features in Irish, but in my opinion by far the most accomplished of us men was Niall Tóibín. Niall was a scholar of the language. He spoke mellifluous Munster Irish, and was equally at home in the other three dialects of Ireland. His mimicry in either language was only delightful. The bilingual actors were the hardest worked in the Rep. Frequently an actor who played the lead in the Sunday night play in English would appear again in the same role in the mid-week play in Irish.

But for pontifical and dogmatic intonation, when God sat on the clouds and spoke in English to the universe, it was in the voice of Joseph O'Dea.

As well as our own producers, outsiders came in. Frank O'Connor came to do a trilogy of his short stories which he had adapted for radio. A resident producer sat with him in the glass box to attend to the technical details. Frank took his eyes off the script and listened to the actors' voices. He noticed that players picked up the pace from each other and tended to sound alike. He got an individual pace from each actor so that their characters were distinguishable to the listener. Because it was his own work the words were never frozen on the page; as new ideas and new ways of saying things struck him, he altered the text, even coming danger-ously near broadcasting time. Before Frank came in, the actors had already been cast in their parts by the station. Listening to them speak he saw that some were more suited to other roles. I, who had a walk-on part in *The Luceys*, found myself playing the lead. Other actors had the same experi-ence in the other two plays, *In the Train* and *The Long Road to Ummera*. In this last Pegg Monahan created the part of the old woman living in the city who got her wish to be buried in west Cork.

Denis Johnston came in to produce his own plays and in particular I remember him doing a work of great imagination and humour, *The Old Lady Says No!* Mícheál Mac Liammóir was guest artist in the role of Robert Emmet, a part he had created many years before at the Gate. Though he was older now, Mícheál's voice was still young and my fresh green memory is of the way he used that beautiful voice to create a memorable portrayal of an actor in the part of Emmet, who because of a fall on the stage continues through Dublin in the same role, reliving the days before he met his fate in Thomas Street.

One day at rehearsal Niall Tóibín, with his back to the studio door, was regaling a group of actors with a delectable impersonation of Mícheál. The door opened noiselessly behind him and there stood the great man himself. Unaware of his presence, Niall carried on, and the actors facing Mícheál were glued to the ground fearing an outburst of vexation. Mac Liammóir's face clouded momentarily, then cleared, as he realised, I suppose, that imitation was a form of flattery. He gripped Niall's hand and said, 'Dear boy, you are a very good actor, but don't let me ever hear you do that again!' And with a joyful hum through his nose, which was slightly in the air, Mícheál strode out into the corridor.

Many people came in. We rubbed shoulders with the famous — Bridges Adams, Hilton Edwards. But the most notable was Tyrone Guthrie, a man of international repute. He came to produce *Peer Gynt*, which went out live on two Sunday nights. As in Frank O'Connor's case, the play had already been cast for him, but on hearing the actors' voices he recast it. Cyril Cusack was to play the title role, but as he wanted some days off to finish a film, Guthrie dropped him in favour of Chris Curran. Guthrie didn't like the acoustic in the large studio. He wanted a livelier, crisper sound, and the carpets were taken up. Now the sound of the actors' shod feet was picked up by the microphones so he asked them to remove their footwear. Doing it with our boots off was new to us. Most actors brought in their bedroom slippers the next day.

Sound effects on disc he dispensed with. The actors had to produce them vocally. For camels trotting in the desert we hit our open hands against our pursed lips making a pop-pop sound, which seemed to tickle him immensely. Howling winds were a kind of banshee sound. With bass, baritone, tenor, soprano and contralto voices, the winds high and low had great variation.

For a sinking ship there was a large bath of water in which we sloshed about with our hands to give the effect of men struggling in the brine. Drowning sailors filled their mouths with water and gurgled their way to Davy Jones's locker. Guthrie's ideas were so new, so inspired and came so rapidly that you'd swear the Holy Ghost had descended on him. But he was a rigid disciplinarian. His voice had the hard edge of that of a British officer and aroused in my memory cells echoes of peasants being made to toe the line. He was a stickler for punctuality. At ten o'clock he stood at the studio door and tardy arrivals had to answer for themselves. One morning a principal actor was some minutes behind the time and was asked what had delayed him. He replied that he had had a nosebleed.

'Show me your hankie!' Guthrie demanded. The actor did and the rag was red enough to stop the traffic.

At ten past ten Guthrie saw through the glass Roisín Ní Shé, who provided the harp music, arrive. Putting down the talk-back button, he shouted, 'Mrs Harp, you're late!'

Lionel Day (Lal O'Dea in real life), Arthur O'Sullivan and I were cast as a kind of ancient chorus. If we weren't on the mike dead on cue Guthrie wanted to know what had happened to 'these three old drearies'. He was quite uncomplimentary in his references to the men, and the women too, and had no compunction in using the soldier's word in front of them if things went wrong. But nothing did . . . on the night. The two shows went out on consecutive Sundays and were rightfully acclaimed.

After the second show we had a party in the studio where we all became very pally. Because of a shortage of containers, Guthrie and I drank out of the same glass, what he called 'sup chum'. I remember him telling us that he had been connected with a radio production of *Journey's End* for the BBC. It was before the days when effects were put on disc and all sounds had to be manufactured in the studio. The producer wanted the tramp of marching men for a few seconds at the opening of the play. Extras were employed to mark time in a gravel rectangle in another studio. The red light went on, they were on air, the men were cued and began to march. At the end of the show the producer went to the other studio and there were the men still marching! He had forgotten to cue them out.

Actors are the worst in the world to do party pieces, but that night Arthur O'Sullivan prevailed upon me to tell a humorous folktale I had heard in Kerry. I don't think it meant a lot to Guthrie but he wasn't dismissive. He pronounced it a prime piece of clowning. Mícheál Ó hAodha was at the party and asked me if I had many more stories like that. I had, and he gave me a spot on Din Joe's *Take the Floor*. Like Guthrie's *Peer Gynt*, it was a success and that was the start of my storytelling career.

7

THE RAMBLING HOUSE

Din Joe's *Take the Floor* was the only radio programme with dancing. Dancing on the air seemed in no way odd at the time. The rat-a-tat-tat sound of the Rory O'Connor troupe was refreshing, and was achieved by the tapping of well-shod dancing feet on thin wooden laths backed with strips of canvas – a little like an extended roll-top desk cover. The laths moved under the dancers' feet and made an unbelievable clatter lifting off the floor. Rory O'Connor was the foremost dancer of his time and had the doubtful distinction of having danced for Hitler during the 1936 Olympics in Berlin.

One night in 1956 I had a story in *Take the Floor* about the Killarney man who fell into the bottomless Devil's Punch-Bowl and came out in Australia. To which Din Joe added, 'He walked down the road to Melbourne and was just in time to enter for the swimming competition in the Olympics!'

By this time, 1956, electricity on tall ESB poles had marched into the remotest valleys and people were able to dispense with their (only for the news) dry battery sets. On the new plug-in radios *Take the Floor* had a huge following in the country, and every new show brought me a sheaf of stories in the post. Not all of them were suitable for the microphone, but many came up trumps in the retelling.

I became so well established that Mícheál Ó hAodha gave me a programme of my own. It was called *The Rambling House* after the houses I knew in Kerry in which people collected at night for news, stories and entertainment. Donnchadh Ó Céilleachair wrote the script and the occupants of the house were singers Teresa Clifford and Seán Ó Síocháin; Éamon Keane recited poems from *Around the Boree Log* and the ballads of Sigerson Clifford. Maura O'Sullivan and Kevin Flood were the son and daughter in the family, who welcomed and chatted with the performers as they entered, exchanging the news of the day and the happenings of the locality. With them I was the man of the house, the *seanchaí*, sitting in the corner adding gems of wisdom to the general conversation and telling a story when my turn came. Albert Healy provided the music on the accordion. As with *Take the Floor*, we had listeners throughout the land and across the sea in Wales.

Because of our radio popularity we actors were invited to perform at functions in Dublin and elsewhere. Ulick O'Connor introduced me to the Bohemians, a brotherhood who met in Jury's Hotel in Dame Street every Tuesday evening. A condition of one's membership was the ability to sing, make music or otherwise entertain. There I learned to work with a live audience and endeavoured to perfect the art of timing. Éamon Keane was invited to the Donegalmen's Association one night, and in the course of his party piece Neil Blaney, the then Minister for Posts and Telegraphs, passed some remark about Radio Éireann at which Éamon took umbrage. One word borrowed another and the upshot of it all was that Éamon was dismissed from the Radio Éireann Players and ordered to go back to the civil service from which he had been seconded.

Éamon refused and went missing. Somebody wrote somewhere that his associates didn't stand up for Éamon. Nothing could be further from the truth. *The Rambling House* was taken off the air as a protest at his treatment. Conor Farrington and I searched Dublin for him and finally found Éamon in An Stad, a Republican lodging house in Frederick Street off Parnell Square. We gave him his weekly cheque, which had lain uncollected in the Green Room.

We advised him that the best thing to do would be to rejoin the civil service and, when the storm blew over, wheels could be set moving within wheels to get him back to the Rep again. He wouldn't hear of it. He was angry at his treatment but he didn't blame Neil Blaney. He thought the decision to sack him was that of some official in the government department showing a little muscle. The next thing we heard was that Éamon had gone to England. He remained there for a while until he came back to Cork to take part in his brother's play *Sharon's Grave*. He worked on the stage for a time and then, as Conor Farrington and I had predicted, he was taken back in the Rep where he remained until he retired.

Without Éamon Keane *The Rambling House* was not revived. Later Mícheál Ó hAodha had the idea of bringing together Seán Ó Riada with his famous orchestra, Ceoltóirí Chualann, the singer Sean Ó Sé and myself in a programme called *Fleadh Cheoil an Radio*. The music, singing and storytelling proved a successful combination and it ran for ages. We taped the programmes in the O'Connell Hall opposite the Gresham Hotel and if we had some minutes to spare between rehearsal and the time of recording, Sean Ó Riada and I went across to the hotel and had a cup of tea — nothing stronger before a performance. Sean, who gave a new lease of life to Irish music, was one of nature's gentlemen. He was high good company, a keen observer of humanity in all its moods and ridiculous tenses. He had stories he had heard from his mother and in the Coolea gaeltacht where he lived. I was welcome to use whichever stories of his suited my book, and very welcome they were, for at this stage I was running out of material. And I told him so.

'When hard pressed,' he said to me, 'why don't you do what de Valera does — go to the country!'

I took to the roads and of all the places I halted, Gougane Barra in west Cork was the best. It brought flooding back to mind all that went on in my own district when I was growing up. Dinny Cronin, the proprietor of the hotel of that name, sent out word when I was in residence, and the neighbours arrived at night and sat in the big kitchen behind the bar and in front of a roaring fire. They were, as the man said, taking the legs off one another to tell me stories. Dinny, rising after putting a sod on the fire, would set the ball rolling.

'There were these two women west here in Kerry. One of them was going to town and the other one was coming from town after a heavy night's rain. This was away back in 1922 when the I. R. aye were fighting the I. R. ah and all the bridges were blown down, and people had to ford the river to go to town.

'The woman going to town said to the woman coming from town, "Were you in town, what time is it, what price are eggs, is the flood high?"

'The fleetness of a woman's mind when it is in top gear! And as quick as lightning the woman coming from town answered, "I was, two o'clock, one and fourpence, up to my arse, girl!"' — at which point Dinny would hit the patched backside of his trousers a most unmerciful wallop.

Dinny claimed that the Free State soldiers were the first to bring bad language to Kerry. 'They were billeted in a certain village not a million miles from where I'm sitting, and a private soldier took a woman's bucket without her permission. He wanted it for drawing water from the well or something. An officer saw what happened and, wanting to keep good relations between the military and the community, ordered the private to return the bucket to the lady and apologise for taking it. The soldier took the bucket back to the woman and said, "Here, Mrs Tuckett, here's your bucket and fuckit I'm sorry I took it!"'

One night as the rain came down in bucketfuls the conversation turned to St Patrick. According to one man, when the saint had converted the Irish they became curious as to how the world would end. St Patrick told them it would go up in a ball of fire. His listeners didn't like one bit the idea of being burned alive, and they wanted to know if the saint could save them from such a catastrophe if the end of the world came tomorrow. (Still the rain came pouring down, which drove one wag to remark that if the end of the world came tomorrow the place'd hardly light! He was called to order and we got back to the narrator.) The holy man pondered the people's question and after some consideration told them he would give them a pledge that God would drown Ireland a year before the end of the world. The people were pleased with that. If they had to go, drowning was a better end than being burned alive! At this point the wag got up to go home and when he opened the door you could hear the rain lashing down on the corrugated iron roof of the cowshed. He poked his head back into the kitchen and said, 'It looks like as if St Patrick is keeping his promise!'

The cottage where the famous Tailor Buckley and his wife Ansty once lived was only a short distance from the hotel, and Dinny had many of the Tailor's stories. According to Dinny, a wealthy farmer put an overcoat making to the Tailor.

The farmer after a few days came for a fitting. He liked the way the job was turning out, and as he had the money handy, he paid the Tailor. When the coat was finished the rich farmer didn't come for it. The weeks and the months went by and winter arrived and at last the farmer came for the coat. But there was no coat. The Tailor had given it to a raggedy poor man going over the hill into Kerry on a cold night. 'It struck me,' the Tailor told the farmer, 'that he needed it more than you! Didn't our Lord say to clothe the naked!'

'A man died sitting on a chair,' Dinny said one night, remembering a Tailor story. 'Dammit if rigor mortis didn't set in, and when it came to waking him he couldn't be straightened out on the table, and a sitting corpse could look bloody awful comical. One neighbour thought of a plan. He tied down the corpse's feet under the table and put another rope hidden by the habit around the dead man's chest. A couple of men put a good strain on the two ropes and secured them well. When he was straightened out if he didn't look as fine a corpse as you'd see in a day's walk. As the night wore on people came to the wake. There was plenty to eat and drink there. Too much drink, maybe, for in the middle of the rosary a blackguard got under the table and cut the rope around the dead man's chest.

'The corpse sat up like a shot, saying "Ahhh" as the wind escaped from his stomach. There was a gasp of horror from the mourners and they skidoo-ed out the door the same as if the plague had hit the place!'

Even though the people in the kitchen had often heard the story before, there was a big hand and praise for the storyteller. Listeners often joined in with words of encouragement during the story such as *'Maith thú!'* ('Good on you!'). On his uttering a truism they'd say *'Is fíor dhuit!'* ('True for you!'). Or telling of some terrible tragedy someone'd say,

'*Dia linn go deo!*' ('God be with us forever!'). When the storyteller made a very telling point the audience would all chorus, '*Go mba slán an seanchaí!*' ('May the storyteller prosper!').

To Dinny I was always the *seanchaí*, and he'd greet me when I arrived with one of the jingles which used to introduce my own programme on the air:

Lift the latch and walk straight in,
There's no better place for glee.
You are welcome to the Rambling House
To meet the *seanchaí*!

The first night I came to Gougane Barra he brought my bag upstairs. There was an occupant already sleeping in the room. Throwing down my bag, Dinny said, 'That's your hammock and that's a hoor of an Englishman in the other bed!' To call me in the morning Dinny threw pebbles from the loose gravel of the yard at my window and shouted, 'Get up, *seanchaí*!' Dinny was as famous a character as the Tailor Buckley. He hadn't as many stories as the Tailor, but he felt that his mission in life was to put me in touch with those who had. He took me in his car at night to farmers' kitchens all over the parish where people gathered to talk after a day's work. I was as welcome as de Valera, a small God there then, and who had had a safe house in nearby Gortaphludig during the civil war. I told tales, some tall tales, and heard tales, some taller. I had to cast a sprat to catch a salmon. I came home with my head bulging with stories and ideas for many more.

I went to Dinny's mostly in the winter when there were no tourists to distract the locals or take up Dinny's time. He had no staff in the winter and he and his wife Nellie saw to my simple needs. Seamus Murphy the sculptor told me that he took Milan Horvat down to Dinny's hotel in the middle of winter. Horvat, a Hungarian I think, was the conductor of the Radio Éireann Symphony Orchestra. It was playing in Cork and Seamus was given the job of showing the conductor the hidden Ireland so he brought him to Gougane. Dinny showed them into the sitting-room. He knew Seamus well. Seamus had been to the Tailor's cottage and had made a now famous bronze bust of that storyteller. Seamus introduced the conductor to Dinny without mentioning the man's occupation. Dinny sensed the imperial foreignness of Milan Horvat and was as curious as hell to know 'where he came out of'.

He set about putting down a fire, a gesture of welcome, spattering talk all round him as he brought in papers, sticks and sods of turf. Every now and then he cast an eye in the direction of Horvat, who was standing by the picture window: a tall, aloof man in a long black coat, holding a fairly wide-brimmed hat behind his back, his eyes taking in the treacherous and dramatic sky tinged with red, the mountains, the lake and the monastic ruin on the island, seeing them we may presume in musical terms. The fire wasn't lighting for Dinny and he took off his cap to blow it as Seamus sat beside him. Finally Dinny's curiosity overcame him and nodding towards the window he said to Seamus, 'Who's this hoor?' Seamus, grateful that Horvat didn't get the significance of the word, explained that he was a conductor. Dinny eyed the stranger, and with a modicum of incredulity enquired, 'On the buses in Cork?'

In Milan Horvat's eyeline across the lake was Timmy Callaghan's house. During my visits to Gougane, Timmy and I became firm friends and I was invited to his house. I am still not sure whether he expected me to believe all the things he told me. Timmy didn't fight for freedom when his age group was out in the hills, but he carried dispatches hidden under the saddle of his bicycle. He was, as he said himself, a handy footballer and played in every position in the field including the mark. Because of a falling off in speed as the years went by, he found himself in the goal.

'We were playing in the final of the parish league,' he told me, 'and the opposing team knowing my weakness placed all the good looking women they could find at the two sides of the goal. Blast it,' he said, 'watching the women I left everything in, and we lost the match!'

Timmy believed in fairies and told me that if you met them they looked the same as you or me. You wouldn't know the difference. Then he continued: 'I went with my own horse and butt to Bantry for fish. I set out the night before, so as to be among the first at the market in the morning. The night was bright except when great banks of cloud scudded across the face of the moon. After some time on my way I put my hand in my pocket and found I had no matches to light my pipe. Around the next turn of the road I saw a fine house all lit up. It must be new, I said to myself, for I hadn't noticed it going to Bantry before. Maybe an ex-policeman built it.

'I tied the horse to the butt of a whitethorn growing on the ditch and went in. A great crowd inside; all strangers to me and they made no wonder of my presence. There was music playing and young men and women dancing as wild and as airy as they would be at the pattern below in Gougane. I filled my pipe as I watched them stepping it out. With the crowd I couldn't get near the fire to light it so I put the pipe on the table in front of me. When the quadrille was over the lady in charge asked for a donation for the piper. I put what loose change I had, a couple of pennies and a threepenny bit, on the table. Some men were slow in parting with their money, and some refused to give anything. An altercation

arose and while you'd be saying trapsticks fists began to fly.
Women screamed as someone blew out the lamp. I gathered
my legs out of the place as quick as I could, ripped the cob
from the whitethorn and drove away.

'Halfway down the road to Bantry I put my hand in my
pocket and found that I had left my pipe behind on the table
in the new house. There was nothing for it now only grin
and bear it. I'd call in on the way home and ask for the pipe.
I did my few commands in Bantry, bought the fish and hit for
home. When I came to the turn in the road, that I may be
as dead as my mother, but there was no house there. And I
couldn't mistake the place. There was the whitethorn tree
where I tied the cob, there were the fresh horse-apples and
the mark of the cob's hooves in the mud. I went in the gap
I had gone in the night before and there on a flat stone was
my pipe and the two pennies and the threepenny bit.

'Who were they, those people I saw dancing in that house?
Were they the fairy horde? Or the people who have gone
before us? Or did I for a short time visit the afterlife?'

Timmy believed in a hereafter for animals and he often
told me about the man who had a grey horse: 'A spirited
animal with a ferocious amount of white in his eye. A high
stepper that left all the traps and sidecars on the road behind
him going to Mass. Very well why, the man died and shortly
after the horse got sick. People would stay up at night with
a sick animal that time. Two neighbouring men were in the
stable, one at each side of the horse. With the handle of a
broom they were massaging under his barrel to bring him
relief from the stomach cramp he was suffering from.

'They were resting from their work when the dead man
walked into the stable. One neighbour was stricken with
terror; the other fell backwards into the manger with fright.
The horse whinnied to his former owner and the ghost put

77

his hand on the horse's forehead. Then he rubbed down along his mane and down his spine to his tail and the horse crumpled up on the floor. The two white shapes of the dead owner and the dead horse floated out the door and away through the night air. A cow in the stall bellowed and the cock crew on his roost in the fowlhouse.'

I left Timmy and walked back to the hotel by the lake shore and thought of the time when the waters parted and revealed another world below. A woman storyteller, according to Dinny, was joined in butter with Timmy Callaghan's grandfather. She was going by the lake with her firkin in the moonlight when she saw the waters part in the middle and lay bare an enchanted land, where the sun shone, the birds sang, the men worked in the fields and there was an abundance of flowers and fruit. She knew if she had a piece of steel to throw into the opening the waters would remain parted, and she could walk down, meet the people, see how they lived, and have another story to tell when she came back.

She remembered the steel tip on the heel of her shoe and she put down the firkin to untie her lace. Taking her eyes off the lake broke the spell and when she looked again the gap had closed. She was left with only what the mind's eye can hold, a picture that would always remain vivid and bright.

It is all of forty years since I first visited Gougane. The men and women who sat in the big kitchen behind the hotel bar and hurried the night are long since gone. They lie in the little churchyard by the lake. May the sod rest lightly on them and on Timmy Callaghan, Dinny Cronin and the Tailor Buckley. Their spirits are somewhere in the skies in a land of fruit and flowers where the air is forever filled with music and the beat of angels' wings.

8

THE STAGE

Not every actor in the Rep wanted to spend his life behind a microphone, but it was very difficult for us to get permission from the radio authorities to work in the theatre. Stage work could clash with the radio actor's performance at night when almost everything went out live. However, in the late 1950s tape became available and the Sunday night radio plays were prerecorded. On these free Sunday nights, and without the knowledge of the station I am afraid, I went off with a party of singers and musicians who had appeared in programmes like *Take the Floor, The Balladmakers' Saturday Night, The Rambling House* and *Fleadh Cheoil an Radio*, to distant parts of the country for a one-night stand.

The pay was small but there was the advantage of working with an audience. Before the era of television personalities, we were the attraction of the hour and we played to packed houses everywhere we went. It gave me a chance of meeting people and many of those I met had stories for me. About seven artists filled the bill: two male and two female singers, a musician, a storyteller and a dancer. A male singer did compère and each performer appeared once in the first half and once again in the second half, but in a different order.

The shows were lively. There was a great reaction from the crowd and sometimes people talked back to us from the audience, offering comments on the proceedings. In Killarney an old woman in the front row, agreeing with some sentiment in my story, hit the floor with her stick and said, ''Tis true for him!' And in Macroom one of our lady singers wore an off-the-shoulder creation and the other an evening gown showing just as much flesh but with shoulder straps. Coming to the end of the night the compère remarked, 'We have time only for one more item and what better way to conclude the evening than with a song from one of the ladies. Which one will I send out to you?' There was a shout from the gods, 'Send out the one with the galluses!'

After the show there was always a party and whether it was distant Cahirciveen, Ballina or Castleisland, we travelled back through the night to be in time for work next day. Watching the white road lines under the lights of the speeding car meant that a reflection of those same white lines rolled over my eyeballs as I tried to get an hour's sleep before going to work in the morning.

Nearing the end of the decade all the talk in Radio Éireann was about the new television station to be set up. At first it was to be called *Cianamharcaíocht* — a 'distant sighting' — before they hit on *Telefís* — a 'ghost seen afar off'! Some people, not as many as expected, were transferred from the station to the new Radio Telefís Éireann. Among them was Meave Conway who took charge of children's television. She asked me to do a series of ten-minute stories for younger people, and on 2 January 1961, after RTÉ's opening night's festivities, my face was among the first to be seen in the regular television schedule at 5.30 in the evening.

I told the stories live, sitting on a chair, with two cameramen who took alternate shots of me. In time one cameraman was dispensed with and later in the series the other one was also given his walking papers, and I was left with the camera fixed in front of me in a studio so small that it was christened the 'confession box'. The programmes were announced that time, not by a voiceover, but by a physical presence. A lady continuity announcer sat in my chair and told the viewers what they were about to see. Then when the title board came up on the screen – where it originated I don't know – and while the signature tune was being played, the lady quickly vacated the chair and I sat into it. The red light came on and I was talking to the nation!

Our two eldest children, Eoin and Brian, were toddlers at the time. I was told that on first seeing my face in the box, they viewed it with an air of incredulity. Then they laughed and began to talk to me, but when I became stern-faced in the course of the story they thought I was 'telling' them to be quiet. In a day or two they accepted me as part of the normal order of things. Now I often meet people facing middle age who, as children, watched those programmes.

I had a story one evening called 'The Cat and the Splinter'. It was about a carpenter who taught his cat to hold a light for him while he worked at night. The splinter was a long sliver of bog deal used as a light before candles were perfected. I got real splinters from a source in the country and was able to show them on camera. I thought it would be a good idea to light one, and permission to do so was given by the director. It would be an improvement on what was virtually visual radio.

A little way into the story I lit the splinter 'and oh my friends and oh my foes it gave a lovely light!' But when I wanted to put it out, the more I blew on it the more it blazed up. A moment of panic! I thought of throwing it away, but I had visions of an enterprise just opened going up in flames.

Suddenly an idea struck me. Maybe I was blowing too hard? I let the light die down a little and then with the slightest puff the flame went out, much to the relief of myself, those in charge and maybe the viewers if they had noticed anything wrong.

Back in Radio Éireann, restrictions on getting off from the Rep were being eased, and actors were let go to do stage and television work. My first television play was *The Weaver's Grave,* adapted by Mícheál Ó hAodha from a short story by Seamus O'Kelly and directed by Christopher Fitz Simon. The piece was rehearsed in much the same way as it would have been for the stage, and when it came to the 'take' three cameras photographed the continuous action and the director selected the shots he wanted for the screen. We already had audio tape on radio; now visual or video tape became available for television and shows could be prerecorded. Before that, live plays on the box could be an alarming experience, with the next scene being feverishly set up in a compartment of a revolve, and the waiting actor already up and doing when he was turned into the camera. It was said that an actor who had to do a quick change wasn't fully into his costume when his partly clothed image burst into the sitting-rooms of the country!

Our play was recorded in sections as the tape was twenty minutes long. If for some reason we had to stop, the action could not be picked up again and we had to go back to the top. We were in the last minute of a tape in *The Weaver's Grave* when a camera on a crane hovering to take an overhead close-up crashed into the end of Malachaí Roohan's bed. There was a gasp from actors and crew, and Arthur O'Sullivan who was playing the character of Malachaí, and was in the bed at the time, gave vent to an expletive which almost drowned out the sound of the impact. After a cup of coffee the scene was reset and with our hearts in our mouths we started from the top again.

Hilton Edwards had been head of drama in Telefís Éireann during those early years. One of his first jobs afterwards was to direct Brian Friel's *Philadelphia, Here I Come!* for the Gate. Maybe he was conversant with my work, I don't know, but he sent for me to look at a part in the play. I read it, we talked about it, he gave me the script and said the part was mine. I applied for and got permission from Radio Éireann to absent myself from the station for the rehearsal period only. When the play was running I was to report for work every day. I was often in a live radio programme as late at 7 p.m. and I had to have a taxi ticking over in Henry Street to make a dash for the stage door as near as I could to half-hour.

We rehearsed *Philadelphia, Here I Come!* in the bar space in the Gaiety Theatre for three weeks, which was considered adequate time for the preparation of a show in those days. Patrick Bedford and Donal Donnelly played the public and private sides of Gar O'Donnell. Maureen O'Sullivan was the housekeeper. I was S. B. O'Donnell ('Screwballs' to Gar Private) owner of the shop, county councillor and father of Gar. Éamon Morrissey played Ned, and Emmet Bergin and Brendan O'Sullivan the other two young men who come to say goodbye to Gar on the night before he goes to America. Dominic Roche was the schoolmaster and Alex McDonald played Canon Mick O'Byrne. Later Mavis Villiers joined the cast as Aunt Lizzie, with whom Gar goes to live in Philadelphia.

Hilton Edwards was a director of the old school, a gifted man of the theatre. He heard the play in terms of classical music, and he saw it in terms of the pictorial compositions of the great painters. The movements, positions and business of his actors he had in his head as he sat down to rehearsal in the morning. An actor was free to suggest a change in these and if it was an improvement it was kept in.

'May I stand over here, Hilton?' an actor might say.

'No, dear boy,' Hilton would answer. 'You'll be in that position in Act Two.'

In interpreting the part of the uncommunicative father of Gar, I fell back on old men I knew in our locality while growing up, one man in particular who rarely spoke when with his own family. At first I was making him too old, senile in fact. Hilton said I was creeping around like a troglodyte, and Brian Friel told Hilton when he came to rehearsal that the man was barely over sixty. I was fifty myself at the time, so a little ageing was sufficient. I got inside the skin of the character and rounded him out till he was redolent of his place on the planet in every respect but one.

Philadelphia, Here I Come! is set in Ballybeg in County Donegal, but Hilton didn't want us actors using a Donegal accent. He was totally opposed to what he called 'regional intonations', and he settled for a clear peasant quality speech which I believe was much in evidence in the early days of the Abbey. As Hilton observed, 'If we ever take this property abroad, the punters of New York or Brighton won't know the difference between a Donegal and a Cork accent. Give them a clear speech. They pay their money and the least they may expect is to understand what's being said.' Accents were never my strong point so I was happy enough with that arrangement, as were many others in the cast, to judge by their expressions.

Under Hilton's tutelage Patrick Bedford and Donal Donnelly perfected a wonderful double act. They were the same person: one was Gar's outward manifestation, the other the inner workings of his mind. Gar Private is not supposed to be heard by the other characters in the play as he reveals what the silent Gar Public thinks about them. To the audience this was

hilarious when handled by these two talented players. In Act
One Bedford sat and felt the lines as Donnelly described my
entrance from the shop to sit down to supper with my son
on his last night at home. 'And here comes your pleasure,
your little ray of sunshine . . . ' Donal introduces me to the
audience in mockingly glowing terms: 'I give you – the one
and only – the inimitable – the irrepressible – County
Councillor – S. B. O'Donnell!'

He hums a fanfare while I hang up the shop keys, check
my pocket watch with the kitchen clock, tilt my hat a bit . . .
Then in tones reminiscent of the catwalk, he says, 'And this
time Marie Celeste is wearing a cheeky little headdress . . .
The pert little apron is detachable!' I marry the action of
removing my apron to his words. 'Thank you, Marie Celeste!'
I dust down my trousers. 'And underneath we have the
tapered Italian-line slacks in ocelot . . . We call this seductive
outfit Indiscretion. It can be worn six days a week in or out
of bed! Have a seat, Screwballs.' I sit. 'Remove the hat.' This
I do and bless myself. 'On again.' I put it on. 'Perfectly
trained. The most obedient father I ever had . . . But hold
it. Hold it.' Here the script says that I take out my handkerchief, remove my upper denture, wrap it in the handkerchief and put it in my pocket.

I had no false teeth to take out and I was in something of
a quandary as to how I could make this piece of business
look credible. Hilton unknowingly solved it for me. At the
time he had put in a set of top dentures, which appeared to
sit uncomfortably on his palate. He champed a little in the
manner of a horse with an ill-fitting bit. He always had the
denture in place, to enhance his smile, when he spoke to us
on the floor, but when he went back to his directorial chair,
he turned his head a little, holding a large handkerchief over
the lower part of his face with his left hand, took out the

offending denture with his right, folded the handkerchief over it quickly and put it in his pocket. An altogether slick operation.

I practised this manoeuvre, taking out an imaginary denture behind the handkerchief, and it went well at rehearsal. As I have the knack of appearing gummy with my teeth in, when I did it on opening night it brought the house down.

A delicate thread runs through the bright fabric of the play. It is a memory Gar has of a day spent with his father in a blue boat on a lake when he was a child, a haunting memory of the two of them together. His father sang, and it must have been raining because he put his jacket around Gar's shoulders and gave him his hat. They were happy. So happy that the thought of it keeps recurring. It comes up when Gar's mind wanders during the rosary. Was it a dream? To know for sure becomes an ache in Gar's heart and, through Friel's beautiful writing, an ache in every heart in the audience.

Philadelphia, Here I Come! was presented at the Gaiety Theatre as part of the Dublin Theatre Festival. *The King of the Castle* by Eugene McCabe ended its run on the Saturday. That night the McCabe set was struck even though it contained a full-size practical threshing machine. Hilton's Gate Theatre company got in later and on Sunday morning the split-level scene of room and kitchen by Alpho O'Reilly was erected. Hilton lit it during the day and next morning was the technical run-through. That afternoon saw the dress rehearsal and we went on stage that night – Monday 28 September 1964. To do all that nowadays the theatre would be dark for a week.

Time has washed all memory of the first night from my mind except the curtain call. The first to move down to the footlights were the lesser players. Dividing each way they made room for the supporting characters, and they, dividing again, left space for Donal Donnelly and Patrick Bedford to walk down to thunderous applause. We held the line and bowed until the punters' hands got sore. Some actors don't read their notices until the end of the run. My curiosity gets the better of me. I read them and they were good, with Donal Donnelly and Patrick Bedford being singled out for their excellent work. All the actors featured in the plaudits, with special mention of Maureen O'Sullivan, Alex McDonald, Éamon Morrissey and myself. Hilton was praised for his superb direction and lighting and Brian Friel for giving us a play that marked a turning point in Irish theatre.

There were one or two dissenting voices. The critic of the London *Times*, talking about John Keane (sic), who like Friel wrote about rural Ireland, said that Keane's characters could translate to Minnesota or Malmö, whereas he felt that Friel's people lacked this universal quality and that therefore his play might have more significance for local audiences than for people elsewhere. Time has proved this man to be as far out as a lighthouse. Brian Friel's plays have turned out to be top box office attractions on Broadway and the West End.

Seamus Kelly of *The Irish Times* loved the play, but wondered why it all hadn't been said before and at the Abbey. Frank O'Connor writing in the *Sunday Independent* quarrelled with Hilton's direction, saying that the wicked magician (Hilton) turned Friel's gentle play into a rip-roaring revue, all sexed-up, chromium-plated and with anti-clericalism. Your humble servant, according to O'Connor, was the only one who never lost sight of Mr Friel. ' . . . Éamon Kelly as the taciturn father allowed nothing and nobody to impinge on his conception of the play, and by the hokeys in the last few minutes when it was lying dead on the stage didn't he get up and give it the kiss of life. As for my friend Hilton Edwards I could personally have beaten him to death with my programme.' O'Connor praised Friel, faulted Hilton and gave me powers of resuscitation which I didn't have, or didn't need, but he ended by saying the performances were brilliant and the audience adored the play.

Professor Liam Ó Briain, in a letter to the *Irish Independent* on 6 October 1964, defended Hilton's direction and said there wasn't a trace of anything that could be remotely described as rip-roaring in his handling of the play. Naming the principal actors, the professor said that they contributed equally to make it a production which for unity of tone was one of the most noteworthy of Hilton Edwards's many noteworthy productions in Dublin.

9

BROADWAY

At a street crossing the traffic lights flashed an urgent 'Don't
Walk'. Hilton Edwards, on seeing this, enquired, 'What do
they expect us to do, run?' Presently a friendly white 'Walk'
beckoned to us in a lamp as big as a television screen. We
were in New York and going to rehearsal. *Philadelphia, Here
I Come!* had been revived at the Gate Theatre in 1965, and
London and New York impresarios, seeing it, arranged for its
presentation on Broadway and later in the West End. The
two leads, Patrick Bedford and Donal Donnelly, were included in the deal, as were Maureen O'Sullivan, Mavis Villiers
and myself. Éamon Morrissey joined us later.

It was a difficult decision for me leaving Maura and three
young children behind. I was every day of fifty-one and a bit
long in the tooth for haring off across the Atlantic. But Maura,
true thespian that she was, gave me her blessing. We agreed
that if the play were successful she and the children would
join me in the States. I got my passport and visa and was
vaccinated, and in the middle of Christmas 1965, after a fond
farewell, more smiles than tears, I got a cab to Dublin Airport.
Hilton Edwards and Brian Friel accompanied the cast on the
flight and to my dying day I'll never forget the sight at twilight

of the New York skyscrapers all lit up like benediction as our plane circled to land at Idlewild. Christmas at home with its candles in the windows paled in comparison to the fairyland that was Manhattan.

All my relations who emigrated came to New York, and from an early age listening to their letters being read and hearing them talk when they came home, New York place-names like Hell's Kitchen, the Bowery, Central Park West and Chinatown were familiar to me. I mentioned this to Brian Friel on the plane and he drew a map of Manhattan with its avenues going north and south and the streets running east and west, and indicated roughly the places I had mentioned.

Our spirits soared that morning as we walked along. The New York air seemed more invigorating than that of Dublin. Everything was livelier. The traffic and even the pedestrians were all hell-bent on getting somewhere fast. Flashing advertising lights competed for our attention and tall buildings, their toenails firmly on the sidewalk, stretched away into the sky.

There was no dining-room in the hotel we actors could afford. We had to go to the corner café for meals. I ordered a boiled egg for breakfast the first morning and got it broken up in a teacup like my mother used to give the baby of the family when I was young. One of the many little things that make America different.

New York actors were auditioned by Hilton for the other parts in the play, and after three weeks' rehearsal we opened our pre-Broadway tour in Philadelphia, which town stays in the memory because the streets were named after trees, and a large statue of William Penn dominated the centre of the city. We played in the Walnut Street Theatre, reputed to be the oldest in America. Sheridan's comedy *The Rivals* opened the playhouse in 1812. It was the great impresario David

Merrick who put on our play and he, his aides and assessors accompanied us on the tour. Actors who didn't measure up to a Broadway standard were replaced and we lost two players on the way to New York.

'Where are you going, Biff?' an aide enquired of another one night in Boston.

'To dressing-room four to fire Louise,' Biff said, I thought with a little relish.

In a while's time a distraught Louise came down the stairs in floods of tears. Without her knowing it, another actress had been understudying the part. Not until we reached New York were some of us free of the fear of hearing that knock on the dressing-room door.

Television stations in Philadelphia and Boston were wont to place a camera before an audience emerging from theatre productions and ask the punters for their thoughts on the play. Merrick disliked this type of publicity as some nut was quite likely to say that the show was a load of garbage. To counteract it he had his crew members, all dickied up, merge with the audience, hog the microphone and offer comments which were laudatory in the extreme. This could only work a few times as the camera people recognised the crew and ignored them. Then Merrick's men played a record from *Hello Dolly*, one of his shows which was running on Broadway at the time, to muffle what was being said. Better still, with a pair of pliers he often cut the leads to the television speaker and left the interviewed playgoers on the screen opening and closing their mouths silently like goldfish in a bowl. He took the pliers out of his back pocket and showed them to us.

David Merrick was described as the *adulte terrible* in *Time* magazine. We were told that once when he got all round very bad notices for a show, he looked up the telephone directory and invited people of the same names as the drama critics to dinner. There were tickets to the panned show, after which he asked the 'Stanley Kauffmanns' and the 'Walter Kerrs' for their views. Quotes from their lavish praise were writ large on the publicity boards in the theatre marquee.

After a week in Philadelphia and another in Boston, where we played in the Wilbur Theatre, we opened in the Helen Hayes on Broadway. There were to be two previews on Monday and Tuesday, 15 and 16 February, and the press night was to be on the Wednesday. At this time there was a row going on between Stanley Kauffmann, the new critic of the *New York Times*, and the Broadway producers. Kauffmann insisted on coming to the second preview because he said the time between curtain down and going to press was too short to write an in-depth review. Merrick's and the other producers' argument was that a preview was not the finished article. Even at the last moment changes could be made which would improve the performance. And anyway, a press night opening was at seven-thirty instead of eight o'clock.

We were in our dressing-rooms getting ready on the second preview night when there was an announcement on the tannoy to get into our street clothes and leave the theatre at once. Outside, a thousand ticket-holders and Mr Kauffmann of the *Times* approached a darkened marquee and a notice saying that the show had been cancelled. Mr Merrick, when pressed for an explanation, said, 'A rat got in the generator.' The cancellation of that night's showing of Friel's play made front page news in New York next morning. Anyone interested in the theatre knew that Merrick had a new play called *Philadelphia, Here I Come!* opening in the Helen Hayes that night.

Being new to Broadway we were nervous, but the excitement of the events of the evening before tended to put us on an all-time high, and we turned in a great performance which received a tremendous reception at the curtain.

Later that night I was walking after Brian Friel on our way into Sardi's Restaurant, a favourite eating place for after-theatre people. When we got inside the door there was a burst of applause. I looked behind to see what famous personality was entering. There was nobody. The applause was for Brian, a warm New York welcome for a new play-wright on Broadway.

We sat up in Moriarty's pub and diner until the papers hit the streets in the small hours. Douglas Watt wrote in the *Daily News*: 'I am happy to report that David Merrick didn't cancel last night's performance of *Philadelphia, Here I Come!* as he did the previous night's.' And he went on to say: 'It is beautifully performed under Hilton Edwards's sensitive direction . . . *Philadelphia, Here I Come!* casts an undeniable spell.'

Walter Kerr of the *New York Herald Tribune* wrote: 'This morning the sun shines brighter. Producer David Merrick has gone window shopping in Dublin and brought us back a fine new play . . . Author Brian Friel has set all of his cranky, fond and obstinate shy people to searching for the word that is everlastingly on the tip of everyman's tongue, and ever-lastingly not spoken. He has written a play about an ache, and he has written it so simply and so honestly that the ache itself becomes a warming fire.'

Stanley Kauffmann's review was not so warm, and didn't merit quotation among the thirty-one excerpts which appear-ed in a full page advertisement in the *New York Times* on 15 February.

We played on Broadway until November. There were many awards for the play, director and leading actors. Brian Friel received a Tony Award nomination, as did Hilton

Edwards for his direction. Donal Donnelly, Patrick Bedford and Maureen O'Sullivan were also named (Maureen had now become Máirín D. O'Sullivan because her name clashed with the famous Maureen in Hollywood), and wonder of wonders, a nomination came to an astonished yours truly. I was pipped at the post for the actual award by Patrick Magee who was playing in *Marat-Sade*.

Many notable people took in the show during its run on Broadway, and we often had to stay on stage to meet them after the curtain. One night Bobby Kennedy and a family party came. The actors crowded around the Kennedys, Bobby's sisters and his wife, and I, not being of a pushy nature, was left in the background. When the party left the stage, still surrounded by the actors, Bobby was last in the line. He stood for a moment and saw me at the far side. I was going to approach him but hesitated. He walked across, shook my hand and said how much he had enjoyed the play. I was very moved by the thoughtfulness of his action.

But of all the notables who came, I think I enjoyed Paddy Murphy's visits best of all. Paddy had been my next-door neighbour at home in Ireland, and I was a schoolboy the morning he set out for America. I remember going to his house to wish him farewell. His departure was in many ways not unlike that of Gareth O'Donnell in the play. His father, as well as being a farmer, was a building contractor in a small way, and Paddy had been helping him and learning the trade. It was a severe blow to the father when Paddy got it into his head to go to New York. The old man was brokenhearted and refused to speak to his son. As Paddy paused at the door the morning he was leaving, to wish him goodbye, his father's only words were, 'You'll be sorry yet.'

Paddy got on fine in the States. He was a motorman on the subway train from the Bronx to Manhattan. Every morning he brought carriageloads of commuters down to the city and carted them home in the evening. He told me he had never seen a Broadway play and was very curious about them when he heard I was going to be in one. I got tickets for him and he rang me up a few times before he came. He had many questions to ask. How long would the play last? Would there be a half-time?

When he came he was so interested in the activities of the household, the naturalness of the people eating, washing up, playing draughts, saying the rosary, the boys dropping in to say goodbye to Gar, that he had to come again to savour what was being said. He told me that it brought him back to his own last night at home, and that the taciturn father 'was my own old man out of the soot'. He admitted to being close to tears. Gar's alter ego puzzled him. He took it that he was a dead brother who came back to advise the young man.

In the following months Paddy organised parties of Kerry neighbours and friends to visit the play. There were so many that afterwards he drew them up in two lines in the wide corridor outside my dressing-room. Then I was called out and marched up and down the lines like de Valera reviewing a guard of honour. He introduced each person as we went along. 'This is Jerry Sheehan from Knockanimeris! And here's a man from Mayo.' (Paddy's wife came from that county.) He read up everything he could lay hands on about the theatre. He became an authority on what was appearing on Broadway and he had sheaves of newspaper cuttings when I called to see him in the Bronx.

I had two aunts and numerous yankee-born first cousins in New York. Sundays were set aside for visiting them. I first called on Aunt Mary at Dittmar's Boulevard in Astoria. I was treated to the same warm hospitality the settled Irish always lavished on greenhorns on their arrival. There was a sumptuous meal and drink to go with it. Generosity knew no bounds. My jacket was put in the closet because of the central heating. On my way home when I looked in the pockets they were full of dollars. There had been a whip-round, what they used to call a 'shower', for the new arrival.

Nearly all the talk on that first visit was about Ireland. How many of the people my aunts remembered were still alive? Marriages of relations at home were discussed and I was questioned about any contributions to the matrimonial fruit basket. Then I was told how my New York cousins were getting on — where they worked and where they lived. Maria, Aunt Margaret's daughter, was married to an Italian police-man. I knew from listening to American relations that marrying outside the ethnic group was frowned upon. Women like my aunts would ask their daughters who were that way inclined, 'What's wrong with Irish boys?' A father giving away his daughter to a Pole or an Italian might say to her at the altar-rails, 'What's that you said his name was again?'

The policeman son-in-law wasn't present on that first visit and I told his wife Maria that as he was on duty in Manhattan he should call into the Helen Hayes Theatre to see me after a Wednesday matinée. Sure enough he turned up with an Irish cop, both of them bedecked with guns, batons, hand-cuffs, parking tickets, whistles, notebooks and pencils. They were hardly able to walk under all that paraphernalia. Actors exchanged curious glances as they saw them entering my dressing-room. I kept a bottle of Irish in my locker and there was a drop all round. They turned out to be a good-humoured pair, and I said for a lark, why not slip the handcuffs on me and frogmarch me out when the other actors were leaving their dressing-rooms. This they did, to the open-mouthed astonishment of my colleagues. They deposited me in the squad car and drove off with one or two hoots on the siren. They dropped me safely at my hotel, where the phone was hopping off the hook. News had spread to the staff of the theatre that I had been abducted by the police. I reassured the staff, and they took some convincing that it was all a joke and that I was available for duty that night. My biggest difficulty was keeping the incident from the ears of the PRO, who would have used it for publicity that would have got two of New York's finest into trouble.

10

LOST IN THE UNDERGROUND

It was March, the play had been successful and the people
were coming in. It looked like as if we'd be in New York for
a while, so I sent to Ireland for Maura and the children. My
first cousin Bob Rodden drove me to the airport to meet
them. It was three months since I had left home, and Eoin,
seven, and Brian, five, had not forgotten me, but Sinéad, a
little over a year-and-a-half, didn't know me at all. She stood
by a railing holding an upright bar, and with her head turned
away she cried her fill. Any word of consolation I had to say
only made her worse. Then I must have had a nudge from
the Holy Ghost or something because I began to hum an
Irish lullaby with which I used to put her to sleep when she
was smaller. Gradually the crying stopped and gradually she
turned her head around, looked up at me quizzically and
began to smile through her tears, as much as to say, 'Ah, I
have you now!'

When we got into Manhattan we discovered that we had
left Sinéad's go-car behind at the Aer Lingus terminal. Next
morning I set out with Eoin and Brian on the subway to
retrieve it. Riding on the underground train was to be a
special treat for them. We had to change trains at a place

called Union Turnpike in Queens. I took Eoin's and Brian's hands firmly when the train stopped. The doors open swiftly and when the people are through they close just as quickly. As we faced the opening door, Eoin, always independent, let go my hand and went towards a door on his right. In a second Brian and I were on the station platform and Eoin, unable to push his way through the entering crowd, was held back by the closing door and left inside. The train sped off and he was gone. The life almost drained from my body with the shock.

My first primitive instinct was to rush after it and try and catch the departing train. There was a coloured man at the window of the carriage and I waved to him and indicated as best I could that I had left the child inside. A lady who had been on our train from Manhattan and noticed the two youngsters with me, seeing my distress, spoke to me very slowly as if I didn't understand English. I was dark and a trifle swarthy and maybe she took me to be Spanish. She asked me to remain exactly where I was and said that she would follow in the next train and see if Eoin had been put out at Van Wyck Boulevard station. She went off and after what seemed like an eternity during which time my brain, veering towards madness, visualised all the dire things that could befall Eoin — would I ever see that dear child again? — the down train drew up and there she was with Eoin by her side. She had found him in the safe keeping of the coloured man. God be praised, I was in the seventh heaven with delight. Eoin, afraid I would tell him off, was inclined to hang back, but I rushed forward, swept him off his feet and embraced him, and when I put him down, my benefactor had gone. On our journey to the airport and back home in the train Eoin clung to my side like a barnacle to the black rocks in Ballybunion.

When news of the incident broke in the theatre the publicity man put me in the hands of a journalist, and a photograph of Eoin and myself appeared with an article in the *New York Herald Tribune*. Heading the article was a verse which read:

Has anybody here seen Kelly,
The kid who was lost and found?
Blessed be the souls who retrieved him,
All in the underground.

Not great. It wouldn't have rated a mention in Radio Éireann's *Balladmakers' Saturday Night*. There was an appeal in the paper to the lady who found Eoin to come forward. Eventually she turned up and David Merrick hosted a dinner in her honour in the Rainbow Restaurant nearly a mile up on top of a skyscraper in Manhattan. Her name was Mrs Francis Koschir and she was the wife of a Jewish doctor from Long Island. She and Eoin were photographed and he had a present for her – an Irish linen tablecloth which Maura found in a New York shop.

I had rented a housekeeping apartment in the Excelsior Hotel at 81st Street and Central Park West. When Donal Donnelly's wife Patsy and their little daughter came to New York they stayed in the same hotel, as did Brian Friel, his wife Anne and their family. We, the Kellys, had two bedrooms, a sitting-room, dining space and a small kitchen. The apartment was cleaned every day and, as ever in America, a mountain of fresh towels put in. We were fourteen storeys up, and when the window-cleaner came I had to close my eyes. He went through the casement and slipped an S-hook from his tackling into a staple on the outside of the frame. The sight of him leaning back into nothingness, singing as he cleaned the window, sent a nervous tingle through my wrists and ankles.

There was a park in front of the building with a planetarium in the middle where we sometimes went to view the stars. During President Kennedy's time a scheme was brought in to cater for preschool children. As Brian was only five he qualified for this and went to the nearest public infant school, where he made friends with kids of every colour in the human spectrum. For his birthday he invited a bevy of them to the apartment and had the time of his life.

Eoin, seven, had been going to school in Dublin and I found a place for him a few blocks away where a one-time Irish parish had flourished, with church and schools all built with the cents and dimes of the emigrants. The neighbourhood was now deepening from white to brown and black, while the stained glass windows in the church still carried an appeal for prayers for the soul of a John O'Brien or an Elizabeth Reidy. Many years later I went to Mass there and the notice on the door said *Misa en Español*. The Irish had gone.

New York streets were very unsafe in the 1960s and children were never left out on their own. I accompanied Eoin and Brian to school every morning and collected them again in the afternoon. Maura did the later chore when I had a Wednesday matinée. Because Eoin would be back in Dublin again to resume his studies, I was anxious that he didn't lose touch with the subjects taught at home. I spoke Irish to him on our way to and from school. After a month or so when he had become accustomed to his surroundings he said to me one morning, 'Dad, I think we shouldn't talk Irish any more.' 'Why so, Eoin?' I asked. 'Because,' he answered, 'people might think we are Puerto Ricans!'

The children enjoyed the strange city although they were

too young for any abiding memory of it to stay with them. Because of their skin colouring as against the pallor of American white children, they caught the eye everywhere they went. Women stopped Maura in the street, curious to know what country they came from, and admiring Sinéad's rosy cheeks they exclaimed, 'Isn't she a doll!' Eoin became very patriotic in the States and hated having to stand in front of the star-spangled banner before class every morning as they all sang 'America the Beautiful'. He told the teacher that it wasn't his flag. I had to traipse around the Irish shops of the city until I found a tricolour for himself and Brian. I have a photograph of the two of them with the Irish flag firmly planted in the ground. With toy guns they defend it against all comers on a small knoll in Central Park.

If Maura and the children enjoyed New York it was a new lease of life for me. In my first days I liked to sit in Schraft's café near Broadway and watch the passing crowds while I partook of a dish of ice cream with scalding hot butterscotch poured on top of it. In these cafés at mid-morning groups of older men with their hats on sat at tables and talked. One day I heard them mention our play and discuss the part I was taking in it. At that time I wasn't hooked on the pint and didn't go to pubs much except to Eddie Downey's of 8th Avenue where showpeople went after the theatre. Eddie had a corner where he displayed pictures of the greats of Broadway and we of *Philadelphia, Here I Come!* figured prominently there.

I rode the subway down to the theatre every night, but when money was plentiful I hailed a cab and asked to be driven through Central Park. The fare was eighty cents and you left the driver the dollar. On the east coast of America spring follows swiftly on the heels of winter. Today the trees are bare; tomorrow there's greenery showing everywhere. I'd spread myself on the back seat of the cab drinking in the beauty of the blossoming shrubbery and, regretting the twelve years I had spent hidden behind a microphone in Radio Éireann's attic on top of the GPO, I'd sing:

> Bless 'em all! Bless Séamus Breathnach
> Who railed us one day,
> 'Will ye stop the bloody acting
> And get on with the play.'

New York cabbies are great talkers and they talk so fast and range over a wealth of topics even on a short journey. One man broached with me the difficulties he was having in his sex life. Mercifully the journey ended before he got to the intimate details.

Reading the name card on another cabman's dashboard I saw Florence O'Donoghue – a Glenflesk name if there was ever one. He turned out to have been the servant boy at Dineen's, a neighbouring farm, when I was a child. I often saw him with a rifle during the Troubles and, because he took the anti-Treaty side in 1922, he lost out and had to flee to America. We were early at the theatre and we sat in the cab and talked about Glenflesk and Killarney until it was time for me to sign on before half-hour. He was saddened by the number of old people I told him had passed on, and agreeably surprised at the many changes for the better in the district. The ride was free. As he said, 'I couldn't take money from a neighbour's child!' Many of the cabmen go to the theatre. One of them asked me, 'Are you the guy who plays the part of the storekeeper in that *Philadelphia* show?'

The Kerrymen's Patriotic and Benevolent Association of New York got wind of the word that I was in a Broadway show and I was invited to their premises to receive an award.

Paddy Murphy went with me. At the door for a joke I indicated that Paddy was my bodyguard. To my surprise this was taken seriously and I was asked if he was one of New York's finest. The term, meaning one of the city's policemen, was lost on me, and winking at Paddy I said, 'Only the finest would do.' Word got around quickly that the tall guy with me was my bodyguard, and I went up in everybody's estimation. We were treated like royalty. When I stood by the podium to hear the citation read, a chair was provided for Paddy in a position where he could cover all entrances and exits. The joke, which Paddy thoroughly enjoyed, had to be played out now, and it wasn't the only absurdity; the one award they had to give was to make me a Kerryman (honorary). And they did just that!

11

SNOWBOUND

IN WILMINGTON AND CHICAGO

The run of *Philadelphia, Here I Come!* came to an end on Broadway and in December we set out on a tour of the States. Our first stop was in Washington where we played in the National Theatre. Our household had a nice apartment there just for one week. I remember the location well because a little distance away on the Y-junction of Pennsylvania Avenue there was a monument by the Kerry-American sculptor, Jerome Connor. It was in memory of the women who nursed the wounded in the civil war. I think they were called the Daughters of the Republic. Down the street from it in the grounds of the Irish Embassy was Connor's statue of Robert Emmet, a replica of which stands in Stephen's Green.

Eoin, Brian and I set out one morning to find a launderette to do our washing. We kept enquiring for one until we were finally directed to a place a distance away in an entirely black neighbourhood. We three were the only white people in the launderette. When I put the clothes in the washing machine I found I hadn't enough coins for the slot. I gave a five dollar bill to a black man and asked him if he would be kind enough to go out and get some change for me. He looked at the note in his hand and said, 'What if I don't come back?' 'You will,' I said, 'your washing is here.' He did come back and we went ahead with the work. As we sat on a bench waiting for the machine to finish, the room filled up. Not all the boys and girls had washing to do – it seemed a kind of trysting place.

I put the damp clothes in the dryer, and after some time an argument started between two people about whose turn it was for the one dryer that was left. Then a strange thing happened. As I was the only white adult there, they assumed I was the owner. I was approached to settle the disagreement. I didn't feel as assured as Aesop's monkey adjudicating between the two cats over the piece of cheese. As they argued their case our dryer gave its last twirl and the swishing clothes came to a halt. I emptied them out and gave one of them the dryer and so peace was restored. I had never before been the odd man out in a crowded room of black people, and because I was new to the States I felt a little uneasy. The children, who saw the world through different eyes, and who had mixed with coloured children at school, were not one bit perturbed.

After our short stay in Washington we were to play for a week in Wilmington, Delaware, and then on to Chicago for two months. Through friends of ours in that city we had already found an apartment, and instead of coming to Wilmington with me, Maura and the children went on to Chicago to await my arrival there on Christmas Day. In Wilmington we played in a theatre in the Dupont complex, and you couldn't ask for nicer weather as we drove there for our last show on Christmas Eve. Back in Dublin all theatres were closed on that day, and in Holy Week the stages were as dark as the words of the Passion on Good Friday. That year Christmas Eve fell on a Saturday and we had two performances, one at five and one at eight. For these back-to-back shows, as they were called, a meal was brought into the theatre, and in the short time before the next curtain-up we didn't have to get out of our costumes or make-up.

Like the first house that afternoon, the second one was a packer. I couldn't help wondering, remembering what Christmas Eve was like in my young days in Ireland, if the people had any homes to go to, or any decorations to put up for the festive season. As the play progressed I found it hard to keep my thoughts from wandering back across the sea to Christmases long ago. There is a scene at the opening of the third act where the family kneel down to say the rosary on young Gar's last night at home before leaving for America. As the Our Fathers, the Hail Marys and the responses swelled and died the thoughts of Gar Public, articulated by Gar Private, always soared westwards across the Atlantic as he visualised what his new life would be like in Philadelphia. But on that night, in Wilmington, as the young would-be emigrant's thoughts soared westward from Ireland, my thoughts were soaring in the opposite direction, to my own home in Carrigeen, Glenflesk.

How clear it all became to me, every detail of the kitchen, the picture of the Holy Family, the berry holly, laurel and ivy decorating the walls. The mottoes on the chimney breast, the roaring fire and the Christmas candles in the windows bringing what was to us then a glorious blaze of light. Images of Christmas crowded the mind. Driving to early Mass in the dark in the pony and trap. The sound of hooves on frosty roads, the loud salutations at the chapel gate as neighbours exchanged Christmas greetings, echoed and re-echoed in my head. 'Your decade!' from the housekeeper, Madge, brought young Gar back from his dreams and me back to reality. The reality that was S. B. O'Donnell's stage kitchen in Wilmington, Delaware.

When we came out of the theatre that night the city was blanketed in snow and strangely quiet, as whatever traffic there was seemed to glide soundlessly over the white streets. We had some trouble in getting a taxi. Those at the centre were lazy about venturing to the outskirts in case they couldn't come back. The snow was coming down again and slanting in the rising wind. Eventually we got an empty cab going in our direction. When we got out the last man was lucky. He stepped into the footprints made by the others in the deep snow which was being tossed and swirled in the wind and driven against the walls of the motel. I had to brush it away to find the door handle, and when I opened the door inwards there was a wall of snow almost three feet high between me and the room.

By scooping it outwards with my bare hands, a bit like a rabbit setting about making a burrow, I managed to get in without bringing too much snow with me. I'll never forget the feeling of loneliness that came over me as I shut the door that Christmas Eve and looked around the bare motel room. Granted, the bed was comfortable. There was a dressing table, a wardrobe, a john and a shower; but one picture would have brightened the place. Just one picture with a sprig of berry holly behind it. I got into bed but I couldn't sleep because of the noise the blow-in hot air apparatus was making. I switched it off but then it got so cold I had to switch it on again.

The phone rang. A fellow player, Éamon Morrissey, who couldn't sleep any more than myself, had rounded up some American and Irish actors from the cast. Would I come down to the lobby? We made ourselves comfortable in a large room and, despite the lateness of the hour, those of us with wives and families called them to send festive greetings. Parcels of good cheer for dear friends in Chicago were raided, and as Christmas Eve merged into Christmas Day, toasts were drunk, songs were sung and on Éamon's insistence I told of Christmases long ago when the world was young and we were all happy by our own fireside.

Next morning at an early hour we were on the road. The snowploughs had cleared our way to Philadelphia Airport, where we were to get the plane to Chicago. Flame-throwers were used to clear the snow from the runway. I got a window seat in an aircraft packed with people, parcels and hand luggage, bursting at the seams like the bus from Killarney to Barraduv on Christmas Eve. It was nightfall when I reached the apartment in Chicago and was united with my family. We exchanged presents and had a quiet drink but it was Christmas Day and I hadn't been to Mass. Maura was anxious that I should talk to God before we sat down to our festive dinner. I went down to reception and was directed to a church in Clarke Street, the scene of the infamous St Valentine's Day Massacre in the time of Prohibition.

Brian and Eoin, full of curiosity about the trip, wanted to know if we brought the stage all the way from the east coast. I told them that in Wilmington on Saturday night coming near the end of the show we heard murmuring in the wings. The men of the theatre transport company were waiting and when the curtain came down they descended on the set like locusts and everything – flats, furniture, lighting-board, wardrobe and props – were quickly put in the vehicle reversed into the back of the stage. They were in the lorry in no time and driving through the night, and whatever time it took them to get to Chicago, that set would be in place and lit for us to walk through before we went on tomorrow night.

Closing in Wilmington on Saturday and opening on Monday in Chicago, nearly a thousand miles away, was, they agreed, something of a record.

Chicago is the Windy City and the coldest place on God's earth in the winter. The icy breeze blowing across the frozen waters of Lake Michigan would be hard on a brass monkey. The nose, ears and the point of the jaw go numb and turn blue, and the tips of the fingers, even in mittens, tingle with pain. The Wilmington snow soon made its way westwards and we woke one morning to find the snow so deep in the streets that parked cars humped the white blanket like knees-up in a bed. The car antennas stuck out of the snow like the stalks of plants waiting for leaves to grow.

One afternoon I had to make my way to WFMT, a Chicago radio station, to talk on a programme giving publicity to the show. I was well wrapped up for the trip and wearing overshoes which came above my ankles. They weren't high enough and the snow went in over them, adding greatly to my discomfort. While waiting in the anteroom at the station, I took off my shoes and put my socks on the radiator. Unnoticed, I hope, I slipped my feet into my wet shoes when I was called. Once my legs were under the studio desk I discarded the wet shoes and I was interviewed barefoot by the legendary Studs Terkel, author of *Division Street: America*. His book was a collection of his most successful interviews, and one authority said of him, 'Studs Terkel is a wonderfully skilled interviewer, with an instinctive ability to put the question that unlocks defences and coaxes self-revelation!'

About this time Spoken Arts of New York had issued a record by the Radio Éireann Players of two plays by J. M. Synge, *Riders to the Sea* and *In the Shadow of the Glen*. The actors' names for some reason did not appear on the sleeve of the album. As I entered the studio an excerpt from *In the Shadow of the Glen* was on the monitor and going out over the air. You could have knocked me down with a feather when I heard my own voice, and Studs was equally surprised when I told him he was listening to me and my wife Maura on the disc. To put his hand on that particular record was a chance in a million and it gave us something to talk about at the opening of the interview.

Studs himself spoke very little but he had the uncanny knack of drawing speech from his subject, and I talked about radio and theatre in Dublin, the play I was in, storytelling and the place where I grew up in Kerry. When it was over I slipped my feet into my shoes and when I came to the anteroom my socks were dry on the radiator.

But we weren't finished with the snow. After a two-month run in the Schubert Theatre in Chicago the tour was to continue with one-week stands in nine other cities throughout the States. We thought the constant changing would be too much for Maura and the children, and after due consideration they decided to go back to Ireland. They had been almost twelve months away. It was a glorious morning when we set out for O'Hare Airport. I wanted to see them off. I would be back in plenty of time for the night show. Our cab driver was Italian, newly arrived but with a fairish grasp of English. We weren't long on the road when the skies darkened and it began to snow. In no time it was coming down thick and fast with fat snowflakes falling on the windscreen. The wipers worked for a while and then failed to function. We had to stop every now and then to clear the soft snow from the glass.

When we got near the airport the snow was so deep that cars were being abandoned on the roadway. A little further on, the thoroughfare was completely blocked and the driver

decided to turn around. He reversed into a ditch where the
cab got stuck and we were marooned in the snow. This was
before the time of telephones in cabs and he went looking
for a kiosk to call his company. We were all in our light
clothes and we soon began to freeze. The driver didn't come
back and I stood in the road to the city flagging down traffic
in the hope of being taken back to Chicago. At last when I
was nearly frozen to death a car stopped. It was a minister of
religion. Little Sinéad was so cold that he opened his
greatcoat and put her inside it while he shepherded us into
his car.

He said he knew a back road to the airport and he took
us there. We were far from the departure area but we found
sheltered accommodation with many other stranded people.
All Maura's cases were in the cab, and in the cold and
excitement of being rescued from it we forgot the hand
luggage with her tickets and passport. Now panic really set
in. How could we trace the cab driver? We asked for the
airport police, and when they came they were flabbergasted
to learn that Brian, not yet six, and having an obsession with
figures, remembered the registration number of the stranded
cab. We gave the police all the particulars, how many pieces
of luggage and the names on the destination tags. They went
off.

In the blizzard there was no hope of my getting back to
the city, and now the full horror of the situation dawned on
me. I was going to miss the show that night. I tried in vain
to ring the theatre. I calmed myself down by saying that it
wasn't a total disaster. We were all alive, and what were
understudies there for but to go on in an emergency? Eoin
and Brian came to the matinée at the Schubert with me every
Saturday. They read their comics in my dressing-room and
listened to the show on the tannoy. Now my mind was taken

off the concern of the hour listening to Eoin talking to a group of truck drivers sitting nearby. Remembering some dialogue from the play, Eoin asked these disgruntled men, 'Why does a hen cross the road?' I had to smile. The incongruity of it. A child of seven engaging the attention of these hardened veterans of the parkways. I thought they'd tell him to scram. But no, they wanted to know why. Eoin told them, 'To get to the other side. Ha-ha! Why does a hen lay an egg?' They hadn't a clue. 'Because,' Eoin said, 'it couldn't lay a brick. Yo-ho. Why does a sailor wear a round hat?' They feigned puzzlement, then said, 'Put us out of our misery, kid.' And Eoin capped his own question with 'To cover his head. Ha-ha!' He had run out of dialogue and returned to us.

After what seemed ages the police came back to say that the cabman had succeeded in being hauled out of the ditch, and when the traffic eased he delivered our luggage to the Aer Lingus terminal. Much relieved by this news, although regretting that I didn't have the opportunity of paying the cabman in whose debt I would ever be, we went to the pilots' lounge where there were easy chairs in which we could rest. Later on we were taken by airport car across the runway to the departure area. We checked to find that tickets and passport were safe, but learned at the desk that because of the snow all flights were grounded until tomorrow.

We had a meal in the restaurant and a generous member of the Aer Lingus staff gave us his apartment a distance away. How great is the goodness of human nature! There was one double bed, and worn out from the day's adventure the entire family got into it. After a while the children complained that there wasn't enough room and they were being crushed. They pushed and pushed until I fell out on the floor where I spent the rest of the night.

Next morning, with the luggage checked in for the flight and Maura and the children sitting in the lounge by the departure gate, we said our tearful goodbyes. I left them bound for Ireland, while I headed back to Chicago. There is a stiff fine levied on any actor missing a show in the theatre, but when I explained my case to the management, they held that my absence was caused by circumstances outside my control and I was forgiven. They were happy enough; my understudy had gone on and the performance had been a success.

I wish I could report that things had gone so smoothly for Maura and the children. According to her first letter, their plane, after many delays, took off from O'Hare Airport. Some trouble developed when they were over Canada and they had to make an emergency landing at Montreal. The passengers were taken in buses with a police escort – they had no landing papers – to hotels in the city, and after an early start the following morning they were only a short time in the air when another fault occurred, something to do with the undercarriage. They circled the city several times and came down so low they could see the ice in the St Lawrence River. Because of the long delays due to bad weather at Chicago Airport and the emergency landing at Montreal, many of the passengers were distraught and being comforted by the ever-attentive and kindly flight staff.

Finally the fault was rectified and the plane straightened out on its flight line to Ireland. Later Maura had a letter from Aer Lingus congratulating herself and the children for remaining so calm under the trying circumstances at the outset of the journey. Happily for them they were at home in Ireland and we actors were on our way to St Louis on the banks of the Mississippi.

Our hotel there was close by the river and we watched

the big-wheeled paddle boats dock and then sail on. Some of us took the elevator up the inside of the chromium-plated twin arches that have become the trademark of the McDonald's fast food outlets. The view of the city and up and down the river was breathtaking. Modestly hiding away in a corner not far from the braggart arches was an elegant little Catholic church going back to the time of the French.

I haven't mentioned the play reviews we got on the road. They were first class. We won all the way. Bob Goddard of the *St Louis Globe-Democrat* exclaimed, 'Where have you been all my life, Mr Friel? That is the natural question after a viewing of a memorable stage experience called *Philadelphia, Here I Come!*'

And so the word was in Columbus, Ohio, and over the border in Toronto where we played in the Royal Alexander Theatre. We went on to Cincinnati, Cleveland and St Paul, and our prop money was stolen in Milwaukee. The people in the design department were put to the pins of their collars to dream up imitations of three green Irish pounds, a foxy ten-shilling note and two half-crowns. They did it and the secretary of the Department of Finance in Dublin wouldn't have known the difference from the front row.

Our travels brought us back again to Boston where a critic sporting the name of Kevin Kelly gave us what I can recall as the only bad review of the play. 'It failed to move me,' he said, 'and was little more than blathering bathos.' In Philadelphia, where we had also played on the run in to Broadway, I read a review of the show on the way to the theatre on opening night. I imagine that the critic, on seeing that there was little or no change in the original cast, dolled up his review of our first visit and gave it to the editor, who put it in the paper a day too early. It was an eerie experience seeing our names down for something that hadn't yet taken place. In New Haven, Joyce's *Ulysses*, shot in Ireland, was showing at a city cinema. I went to see it, and it was like a visit home. The auditorium was crowded and my seat was at the very front, from which vantage point my actor friends from Dublin looked larger than life.

We ended our tour of America in Baltimore on 13 May 1967. It had been nearly a year and a half since I had left home. In that time I had seen most of the States except the far west and the deep south. At first I thought I wouldn't like America. I had great confidence in socialism then, my face ever turning to the east, and I felt that the screaming ideology of US capitalism would set my teeth on edge. I wasn't long in New York when I became aware of the wealth of Park Avenue and the poverty of Harlem. As the song says:

Though gems adorn the great and grand
There are faces with hunger paling.

In downtown Manhattan I saw poor black women rummaging for food in garbage cans, and people sleeping on the doorsteps in the night-time, something which was not in evidence in Moscow, where I went many years later. In the States the successful white man is cock-of-the-walk, and at that time you'd see no coloured faces in posh restaurants or striding down the concourses of great American airports — unless they were working in those places. On tour out from New York, I felt from the way some of our American crew members spoke to coloured porters in railway stations that in his heart the white man was master, and he still regarded his black brother as a slave. This feeling of superiority manifested itself in unexpected ways. When I got up to give my bus seat to a coloured woman in Columbus, Ohio, all the white people looked at me as if I had two heads.

I was at many parties in Irish American homes, but I never saw a coloured face. The Irish in England have married Asian and African partners, but I never heard of anything like that in the States. The Irish American attitude to the coloured seemed to me to be much the same as that of the majority of our settled kith and kin to the travelling people at home. But what a welcome our American cousins have for their white brethren from Ireland. Their hospitality is heart-warming and their generosity knows no bounds. I found friendship to be the hallmark of all Americans. Brendan Behan said of them, 'He who hates you, hates the human race.'

12

TO BRIGHTON AND LONDON

Before we had set out on tour from New York each member of the cast had bought a tin trunk similar to those returning Yanks brought home in the old days. These stood four feet high and were two feet broad and two deep. When opened out, one side held drawers and the other a wardrobe space complete with coat-hangers. They were transported with the stage scenery and sat in the wings at each venue, and you took what you wanted from them to your hotel.

Now they were being packed for the last time for our journey back to Ireland. My trunk was shipped by sea and I hurried back by air, anxious to see what the home place looked like after seventeen months away. O'Connell Street seemed bare. Nelson's Pillar had been blown down the year before. I regretted this. During the twelve years I had worked upstairs in the attic of the GPO as a radio actor, I was on the same level as the one-armed one-eyed figure. Every day I promised myself that I would climb to the top. I never did. It wasn't the cost that kept me away. The sign at the entrance read 'only 3d'.

The pillar itself was a graceful Doric column reaching into the sky. I can still see the words sculpted on the four sides of the granite base. Trafalgar was there and I remember February and April. These were cut in lower case and the years in Roman capitals. Seamus Murphy the sculptor ever marvelled at the classical proportions of the letters in those words. He held that they were the best example of lettering in these islands. Militant Republicanism is short-sighted. The destruction of the pillar and the equestrian statues of King William and Lord Gough were wanton pieces of vandalism. We should learn to live with our past.

I didn't bring my tin trunk to England. It still sits in the spare room with a large Cunard Line label on it.

We opened our pre-West End tour of *Philadelphia, Here I Come!* in Brighton. Maura and the children came over for a visit and the youngsters enjoyed riding on the toy railway and the many other amenities for young people in the August sunshine. I had a movie camera I bought in New York and I still have pictures of them on the merry-go-round.

Jack Tinker was writing then in the *Brighton Evening Argus* and he spoke of the dewdrop freshness of the play. The English were going to like it. Oxford was our next stop and then into London, but at the last minute Manchester and Golder's Green were added to the schedule because the original date for our play in London clashed with the opening of another show, which meant we wouldn't get our full share of the press.

I had been engaged to take part in a television series called *Never Mind the Quality Feel the Width* with Joe Lynch and John Bluthal playing the leading parts in a joint tailoring business. One was Catholic, the other Jewish, and the comedy in the series arose, as it were, from the collision of these two cultures. I was to play the part of a parish priest, and rehearsals were to begin the week we opened in London when I would be free in the daytime.

Now I couldn't do it because I'd be a couple of hundred miles away. A contract had been signed and there was hell to pay. A proposition was put to me by the Thames Television company. Would I be willing to take a late train out of Manchester each night to London after the show? Without telling my own management of my predicament I decided to chance it. It worked fine for two nights. On the third night I went to the railway station to find that there was a lightning strike. My God! What was I to do? The television show I was rehearsing in London was going out live on Sunday night.

It was difficult enough getting accommodation at that late hour. I found a place, the worst ever in which it was my misfortune to lay my head. The bed was damp and there was a shiny coating of dirt on the bedroom carpet. I had a light overcoat which I wore over my pyjamas between the sheets. I was up at the crack of dawn, got a taxi to the airport and flew to London. I rang the TV people and a courtesy car brought me to rehearsal and back to the airport afterwards for the flight to Manchester.

This is how it was for the rest of the week, and because I was under extreme pressure both the play and the TV rehearsal and broadcast went the best ever. When Oscar Lewenstein and Michael White, the English producers of our show, heard that I was going down to London from Manchester every day, all hell broke loose, because of the risk involved if I couldn't get back for the show. They got after my director Hilton Edwards. Hilton bore down on me like a great three-masted schooner on a small boat. Was it true that I was taking the train from Manchester down to London every day?

'No, Hilton,' I replied. 'I go by plane.'

That seemed to take the wind out of his sails, because he thought for a moment and said, 'You're flying? Well I suppose that's all right.' Strange logic, but it got me off the hook.

After a week at the Hippodrome in Golder's Green we opened at the Lyric Theatre in Shaftesbury Avenue on Wednesday 20 September 1967. At the matinées tea was passed along the seats to the patrons at the interval, and we in our dressing-rooms knew when the time was up by the rattle of the empty cups and saucers being collected by the ushers.

The dressing-room was where I lived when not on stage, and I tried to make it as much like home as possible. There was a couch and an easy chair, a cabinet with drinks in case anybody called round, and I had just one picture. It was a reproduction of Picasso's *The Jester* which I had bought in New York. A white figure with a sad face on a light green background. I regarded it as a sort of talisman. It went with me on tour through the States and It was here in London now.

Outside, the names of the principal actors loomed large on the theatre marquee, and posters of the show were fixed to the wall at pavement level. I was glad that my name was just high enough on the bill that a passing dog with an inclination to raise a leg couldn't reach it. Madge Ryan, who replaced Mavis Villiers and who had a better agent than I, had her name placed above mine, but mine was still safe from the designs of contemptuous London canines. A player whose name escapes me was once asked what he thought of drama critics and he replied, 'You may as well ask a lamp-post what it thinks of dogs.'

But the West End critics were kind to us, though they didn't write about the show with the same gusto as their American brethren. The theme of the play somehow struck a deeper chord with people of the New World. Everyone there of European descent had an ancestor whose last night in his native place was, in many respects, not unlike that of Gareth O'Donnell.

Dominic Roche and Derry Power from the original Dublin production joined the cast in the West End. Dominic, who played the part of the schoolmaster and was no stranger to the London stage, had a story about the Lyric, where we were now. The theatre faces Shaftesbury Avenue, while Windmill Street passes the stage door. An old actor playing there had a short appearance in Act One and didn't come on again until late in Act Three. He had all that time (including two intervals) to kill. Sitting in his dressing-room became boring, and to while away the time he walked each night from his dressing-room, down the long corridor, out the stage door, across the street and into the Lyric Tavern, where he sat on a high stool over a drink and did the *Evening Standard* crossword.

The play had a long run, and with practice he had his return so well timed that, after glancing at his watch, he got off the stool, walked out of the pub, crossed the street, went in the stage door, down the long corridor, into the wings, and without pausing walked on to the stage on cue. The old actor prided himself on his achievement, but one night he was late. Only imperceptibly. It seems when he emerged from the pub a window-cleaner with a long ladder on his bike was going up Windmill Street.

I am in my element in big cities. In them you can fade into anonymity, and there's no Dublin passer-by to say, 'How's the man?' A chap can be as lost with his thoughts in a crowded street as if he were strolling through a woodland glade. There are city parks in which he can sit and run lines to himself, pubs in which to have a pre-lunch drink and art galleries to visit when the spirit needs lifting.

In the long run of a play the actor has the company of his peers at show time. After the curtain, when the goodbyes are said at the stage door, he is on his own until he meets them again the next night. This is when he misses his family, and mine was back in Dublin where the children had started school again.

Living accommodation proved difficult enough to find in London in 1967. Hotels were out of the question on our salaries. I had to be satisfied with a small flat in Cadogan Gardens, a stone's throw from the King's Road. I had never lived alone, fending for myself, and for a fairly gregarious type of fellow it proved lonely. When the door of the flat shut behind me on Saturday night, I wouldn't see a face I knew again until a half-hour before the show on Monday.

Ever heeding my mother's admonition to 'keep the faith', no matter what strange place I was in, I always managed to make Mass on the Sabbath day. On my first Sunday in Cadogan Gardens I had no idea of where there was a Catholic church. From past experience in foreign cities I had learned that the only people afoot early on Sunday morning were Catholics on their way to Mass. That Sunday at 8.45 a.m. I walked to Sloane Square and noticed a sprinkling of people heading in a certain direction. I wondered if they were of my persuasion. Any doubts I had were soon banished on seeing Garret FitzGerald, who was later to be our Taoiseach, striding along. I tagged on behind and, sure enough, we came to a Catholic church in time for nine o'clock Mass.

13

THE ABBEY — A HALTING SITE

Philadelphia, Here I Come! ran for three months at the Lyric
Theatre in the West End. I had been in it off and on from
1964, and continually for almost two years since it had
opened on Broadway at the beginning of 1966. It was time
for a change. Back in Dublin after a meeting with Tomás Mac
Anna, artistic director of the Abbey Theatre, I was cast in
Spreading the News, which was part of a Lady Gregory season
at the Peacock. Tomás himself was to direct it.

The Abbey then was a secure place for actors. They were
all permanent, some of them working together for as long as
twenty years. It was very much like a large family and I felt
an intruder for a long time. I likened the house to a caring
old bird with her brood sitting comfortably under her
protective feathers. But this old bird, though moulting at
times, was true to the ideals of the theatre's founders, and
mostly sang the native song. It was the song heard in the
cities and villages of Ireland. When she sang it well, it was
true and glorious and sent a tingle dancing in the blood. She
faltered only when she sang to a borrowed tune.

When I joined the Abbey in 1967 many young people were
coming in from the school of acting. There was a tendency

then to cast juveniles in oldish parts, which meant a heavy application of make-up. I often thought that the young men's heads tended to bend forward under the weight of grease-paint, revealing necks of a natural complexion.

Each actor had an empty cigar box with a hinged lid in which he kept his sticks of Miner's or Leichner's make-up. The sticks were numbered and the most commonly used were No 5, a yellowish shade put on all over the features as a base, and No 9, a red stick applied over the base where the natural colours were prominent in the face. It was much used for florid, outdoor types, of which there were many in the plays of the time. No 15, a paler red, was mixed with No 9 to tone it down for characters with sedentary occupations. A dark stick, No 7, was used if an actor was in the part of an African or Asian, for example the Indian peddler in Bryan MacMahon's *The Bugle in the Blood*.

By rubbing a pared matchstick to No 7, lines could be drawn to indicate wrinkles on the forehead or at the corners of the eyes. Some actors highlighted these dark lines with a streak of white. But the veterans thought this was overdoing it. Cyril Cusack once said that he spent half his life putting in wrinkles and the other half obliterating the natural ones. There was lake, a dark red stick, which was applied above the eyes to set them back, because the old form of stage lighting tended to flatten the face. Lake was also used around the mouth.

Some placed an eye-liner under the eye and put a dot of carmine in the eye-duct with a hint of white underneath. An old actor told me this was to give a little eagerness to the face. The entire make-up job was dusted down with a face powder, and Fuller's earth was used to grey the hair.

A complete set of make-up was costly, and actors entered it in their expenses sheet when making out their income tax returns. One young man fresh from the day job had no make-up. He borrowed it from his fellow players. One asked him when he was going to buy some of his own and he replied, 'I'm waiting to see if I'm going to be kept.'

Cadging make-up was not unknown and there was a tight-fisted thespian who went for ages without buying any. He had an empty cigar box with a hinged lid from which he had cleverly removed the bottom. When it came to the time to prepare for the show, he placed the bottomless container on top of another actor's open box. As they chatted he lifted his lid and helped himself to the other's make-up. When he finished he slapped down the lid and said to his friend, 'Have a good one!'

Tomás Mac Anna's production of *Spreading the News* and Molière's *A Doctor in Spite of Himself*, translated by Lady Gregory, was an outstanding success. Music and song were added to both pieces in the manner of Máirín O'Farrell's treatment of *The Playboy of the Western World* in *The Heart's a Wonder*. 'Opera buffa' one dissenting voice called the concoction.

When King Baudouin and Queen Fabiola of the Belgians visited Ireland later on, *Spreading the News* was revived and presented with J. M. Synge's *Riders to the Sea* and *An Pósadh* by Douglas Hyde in a special gala performance for the royal couple. The No 1 Army Band played the Belgian and Irish anthems. During the interval the bar was cleared and the actors in the three plays were invited upstairs to be presented to the King and Queen.

We were arranged in a huge semicircle and Mícheál Ó hAodha, chairman of the Abbey board, brought the royal couple around, introducing each actor to them. When the royal visitors were in front of me, Mícheál was called away and the King and Queen were left looking at me. I guessed that royal etiquette precluded me from speaking to them. They smiled, and it must have been some impishness in my face that made them laugh. We were politely controlling our merriment when Mícheál returned and introduced us. They passed on, the Queen pausing to talk with Bríd Ní Loinsigh, whose performance as Maurya in *Riders to the Sea* was superb.

Next in line to meet us was President Éamon de Valera. He was being neglected tonight because of the presence of royalty. The President's eyesight was failing then. He walked rubbing shoulders with his aide-de-camp and shook hands with the cast. When he was near me he turned to his aide and said in a low voice, 'Who are these?' The aide told him that we were the actors. With a beam on his face he shook my hand with renewed vigour. I spoke to him in Irish, which seemed to please him because his smile broadened considerably.

The event was widely covered in the papers next day and Seamus Kelly, writing in *The Irish Times*, ended his article by saying that, according to the talk in the foyer after the show, the night was stolen by Bríd Ní Loinsigh's Maurya, by Peadar Lamb's Raftery, and humility almost precludes me from admitting that I was mentioned too.

My first play on the stage of the new Abbey was *The Saint and Mary Kate*, adapted by Mary Manning from Frank O'Connor's novel of the same name. I played the part of a daft carpenter called Grog Mahon. I remember Patrick Murray's scenery had a towering contraption supporting a platform on which I did my work. Every night I had to climb up to it in a blackout. It was an unnerving experience. I dreaded missing my footing in the dark. The trick, I found, was to make a mental picture of the object and its direction from the wings while the light was on it. Then let your guardian angel take you by the hand when darkness fell.

The play was set in a Cork city tenement called the Doll's House. Frank Grimes and Bernadette McKenna played the young lovers. For this production, director Frank Dermody brought the new Abbey stage mechanism into effect. You had lifts coming up and going down with the actors at the end of a scene, in the manner of Tommy Dando at the organ in the Savoy Cinema. On a night on which the punters were slow to applaud, when our hands were out of view in the descending lift Frank Grimes and I clapped loudly and the applause was taken up by the entire house. Hard enough having to play to them without having to do their work as well.

I grew to love playing in the Abbey Theatre, although you'd get better acoustics in a ball alley. Actors had to keep their voices above the normal projection level or those sitting under the balcony would never know how the story was going. Much as I liked the work, opening nights down the years proved something of a disappointment. It has long been the practice for managements to paper the house for these occasions. Who were invited? Friends of the theatre, I suppose. Shareholders and board members, many from the press, people likely to give publicity to the event. A sprinkling from radio and television. Somebody seeing a group of RTÉ personnel going into the theatre on opening night remarked, 'A pilgrimage to Knock!' There must have been something in that, because a play that got an outstanding reaction from preview audiences could fall flat on its face on press night. On occasion one even sensed a mild hostility out there in the darkness.

After *The Saint and Mary Kate*, *The Playboy of the Western World* was revived. In my earlier years I had played Christy, 'a young gaffer who'd capsize the stars,' but, in the words of the Widow Quin, I had 'aged a score' and now I was cast as Christy's father, Old Mahon. Vincent Dowling was the Playboy, Aideen O'Kelly Pegeen Mike, and Maire Ní Dhomhnaill the Widow Quin. Hers was a superbly gamesome widow, and when she came to coax Christy with, 'Come on young fellow till you see my little houseen a perch off on the rising hill,' she didn't say 'house-een' but gave the word the full gaelicised flavour of 'howish-een' which Synge, the eavesdropper, had heard in Kerry.

Harry Brogan and Mícheál Ó Briain played Jimmy Farrell and Philly Cullen. Tomás Mac Anna, a wizard at moving crowds on a large stage, turned in a spectacular production which went to the Edinburgh Festival. Our venue there was the Lyceum Theatre. This was at a time when national anthems were played before the rise of the curtain. 'The Soldier's Song' was first on the turntable. Not everyone recognised it. Half the audience got to their feet. When those standing saw the other half seated they decided they had made a mistake and began to sit down, but by this time those seated thought it was they who had made the mistake and were now getting to their feet and breaking into what one critic called 'uncivilised hilarity'; and so they went up and down like jacks-in-the-box until all were standing and trying to suppress their merriment. Then 'The Soldier's Song' ended and people were settling themselves and reaching for the chocolates, when suddenly the strains of 'God Save the Queen' filled the house, to be greeted, as the audience struggled to stand, with a hilarity as uncivilised as that which had greeted 'The Soldier's Song'.

The incident did the play no harm and the curtain went up to a laughing audience. One paper next day reproached that same audience for their lack of reverence for 'God Save the Queen', but we got a good press. 'Richness', 'Devastating' and 'Splendours' were some of the headings in the *Scots-man*. 'Synge drew a glorious picture of a browbeaten boy discovering his pride and trying to justify the myth he had created. The devastating climax when hero-worship turns to scorn has been vividly handled by Tomás Mac Anna in this production . . . Vincent Dowling's Playboy was a fine study of bewilderment and bravado. He came out of the night a hunched and pathetic waif and found himself transformed into a hero.'

Other papers praised Geoffrey Golden (Michael James), Mícheál Ó Briain (Philly Cullen), Patrick Laffan (Shaun Keogh) and Máire Ní Dhomhnaill. In the part of Old Mahon I was described by Christopher Small of the *Glasgow Herald* as 'large, hairy, as powerful as a gorilla and much less amiable'. John Calder of the *Daily Mail* said: 'Vincent Dowling as the Playboy and Aideen O'Kelly as Pegeen Mike headed a cast which stormed through a memorable first night like inspired banshees.' And of Harry Brogan's Jimmy Farrell he penned 'the most diabolically comic drunk I have ever seen paralytic on a stage'.

In Act Three of the *Playboy*, at the entry of Harry and Mícheál Ó Briain after getting into 'such staggers' at a morning wake, Harry rattles the latch very noisily. Jerkily the door opens just a little, and one leg, snake-like, investigates the kitchen air before the entire person appears, so full that he is fit to spill. Harry and Mícheál talk about graves and Harry asks Mícheál if he has ever heard tell of 'the skulls they have in the city of Dublin; ranged out like blue jugs in a cabin of Connaught . . . white skulls, and black skulls and yellow skulls, and some of them having the full teeth and some having only but one.'

Here Harry holds up, at the end of an outstretched left hand, two fingers. Eyes shut, he rests momentarily. Then, opening one bleary eye and seeing the two fingers raised, he reaches out with his other hand, as fast as is possible under the weight of drink, puts down one finger and wags the other. It is a marvellous piece of grotesquerie in comic hands with sickle-moon thumbs and never fails to make the house erupt.

He told me once how he came across this piece of business. It seems when Harry came to the Abbey first, Lennox Robinson was directing the *Playboy*. When the actor playing Harry's part came to the 'skulls' speech he was shut-eyed, simulating drunkenness, and he raised two digits saying, 'some of them having the full teeth and some having only but one'. 'But,' Lennox called out, 'you have got two fingers up.' Whereupon the actor opened his eyes and put one of them down, to the amusement of the crew. 'Keep it in,' Lennox told him.

Harry, like the actors of his time, was fond of talking about the old days. Acting is a craft and, like Michelangelo's apprentices, novices learn as much from the master's tales as from watching him perform. But the stage wasn't the be-all and end-all for Harry. He was a committed republican from the way he talked, and the Countess Markiewicz was his heroine. John Bull was the enemy and Harry was reluctant to play in London. 'The heart of a rotten empire,' he called it.

When we were in Edinburgh, Phil O'Kelly, our manager, brought the entire cast to a festival news conference held in the Freemasons' Hall in George's Street. Phil put on what one newspaper man called a *céilí* for the press, by asking the players to do a party piece or talk about the theatre. I told a story which was synopsised in next day's *Glasgow Herald*, and Gabriel Fallon gave a potted history of the Abbey. We would not have an Abbey Theatre were it not for the resurgence of the national spirit at the turn of the century, he claimed, and had it not been for the Abbey Theatre the Easter Rising might not have taken place when it did.

There was vocal agreement from Harry on this, and when he himself got up to speak, with a heavy eye he surveyed his surroundings and said, 'The last time I was in a Freemasons' hall I was raiding it!' He went on to encourage the Scots to engage in a militant nationalism.

14

THE TAILOR AND ANSTY

P. J. O'Connor of Radio Éireann adapted *The Tailor and Ansty* for the stage. The Tailor, Tim Buckley, was a famous storyteller, and he and his wife Anastasia held court in the long winter evenings in their cottage near Gougane Barra in west Cork. Theirs was an open house for neighbours and visitors alike. Eric Cross, a visitor who came to stay for some years in Gougane, wrote down the Tailor's sayings and stories as well as Ansty's badinage. It was meant as a record for the old couples' many friends, but after some excerpts from it appeared in Sean O'Faolain's *The Bell*, the book was published.

The Tailor liked to sing out the title and the name of the publisher, he was so pleased with the project. '*The Tailor and Ansty*,' he would say, 'Eric Cross. Chapman and Hall Limited, 11 Newfetter Lane, London EC4. Eight shillings and sixpence!' Both he and his wife Ansty, God bless them, were as broad-spoken as the Bible, and the book was banned by the Censorship of Publications Board in 1943 as being 'in its general tendency indecent'. But there was nothing in it that I didn't hear from the men sitting by my father's fire when I was growing up.

Stories like the one about the new Department of

Agriculture bull attracted much local attention. People came in such numbers that the owner of the beast decided to charge 6d a head for the privilege of viewing the animal in all its virile ferocity. One man was hanging back from the entrance to the field, and the owner asked him why he wasn't going in! 'I am a poor man,' the prospective viewer said, 'the father of eighteen children.'

'Eighteen children,' shouted the farmer. 'Stand there and I'll bring the bull to see you!'

The animal kingdom interested the Tailor greatly, and he had a story of a mule which died on the way to Cork with a load of butter. The owner, so as not to be at a total loss, skinned the mule and sold the pelt in Macroom. When he came back the mule had revived and was grazing at the side of the road. His master went into a field, killed a number of sheep, skinned them, and while the hides were still warm, applied the fleeces to the mule's body. 'And that animal,' the Tailor told his neighbours, 'lived for fifteen years after with two shearings a year!'

A cat likes fish, it is said, but will not wet its paws, yet the Tailor knew of a cat called 'the moonlighter' that used to fish with its master. Small animals the Tailor loved, even insects, and he told of the *daradaol*, a slow-moving black chafer sometimes called the devil's coachman, because his tail sticks up like a driver at the back of a vehicle. This bucko told the soldiers where our Lord was hiding, and so the animals lost their power of speech because, as the Tailor said, they'd tell out everything.

Irish was Tim Buckley's first language and he was as fluent in that tongue as the poets of Sliabh Luachra. He brought much of the music and rhythm of Irish to the English he had learned. *Glac bog an saol agus glacfaidh an saol bog tú.* Take life easy and life will take you easy. The world is only a blue bag, knock a squeeze out of it while you can, was another saying of his.

The banning of *The Tailor and Ansty* caused a heated controversy in the press and gave rise to a four-day debate in the Senate. In time a new Censorship Board was formed and the book was unbanned, but by then much hurt had been caused to the Tailor and his wife. They, who loved the company of people in their house, were for a time deserted, and worst of all, three priests called on them one day and, forcing the Tailor to his knees on the flag of the hearth, made him burn the book in the fire.

'It was a good book,' the Tailor said, recovering from the humiliation. 'It made a great blaze!' Ansty's only comment was, 'Glory be! Eight and sixpence worth!' That was a lot of money to her.

The Abbey accepted P. J. O'Connor's adaptation of *The Tailor and Ansty*, and it was put on in the Peacock during the 1968 Dublin Theatre Festival. I was cast as the Tailor and Bríd Ní Loinsigh as Ansty. A young trainee director, Tomás Ó Murchú from Cork, was given the job of preparing us for the stage. My experience as a storyteller and my knowledge of the countryside – I was brought up not ten miles from where Tim Buckley was born – helped me to build the character of the Tailor. Bríd and I thoroughly enjoyed the job of getting under the skin of this outlandish old couple from Garryna-peaka. The stories, the bickering, the reminiscences, the jokes, all added up to a fine night's entertainment.

Strangely enough, the Abbey management felt the *Tailor* needed a prop, and put on *The Stranger* by Strindberg as a curtain-raiser. But it was plain to all that the *Tailor* could stand on its own feet. At an early revival, prior to a national tour, *The Stranger* was dropped and the material cut from the *Tailor* script to make room for it was restored.

Bríd and I played in places as far apart as Clonmel and
Cahirciveen. In Clonmel we found ourselves part of the
activities of coursing week. In us you couldn't have found
two less enthusiastic supporters of a sport where ferocious
greyhounds are allowed to hack hares to pieces, and we gave
the Abbey manager Phil O'Kelly a bandle of our tongues, as
Ansty might say, for landing us in such a situation.

We played in an old cinema under the title *Destry Rides
Again*. The proprietors had forgotten to take down the sign
of the last picture. In Cahirciveen there were no toilets
backstage. We had to go down a rickety ladder to a turf shed,
and our dressing-rooms consisted of an old caravan parked
at the back of the Kingdom Cinema. When I sat downstage
to talk to the audience, the audience talked to me.

Arriving in Scarriff, County Clare, we found the hall locked
and the caretaker couldn't be found to let us bring in the set
and props. After many enquiries it was revealed that he was
cutting turf many miles away and had taken the key with him.
Here, as in Cahirciveen, there was no house of lords backstage. Cast and crew were expected to use a hedged-in parcel
of land at the rear. There were up-to-date facilities for the
patrons at the bottom of the hall, but wild horses wouldn't
drag an actor through the audience after he is in costume
and make-up. I procured a large empty paint tin which took
care of the minor necessity.

Leslie Scott, our lighting man, did a brilliant job in getting
us properly lit, providing authentic looking 'turf' fires and 'oil'
lamps as well as arranging that all house lights would go out
as the curtain came across. In *The Tailor and Ansty* I had
long solo passages where I told Tim Buckley's many stories
or discoursed upon 'Lollipopus', which was what he called
Halley's fiery comet speeding through the sky.

On the first night in Scarriff there was one light which

didn't go out. It was a bare bulb under the balcony which lit up the entire bottom of the hall and was very distracting because of the arrival of latecomers. I was surprised that Leslie Scott, meticulous man that he was, hadn't it under control. I soldiered on, my concentration wearing thin, until suddenly, nearing the end of Act One, the light went out.

I rushed around to Leslie to ask what had happened. He told me he couldn't find the switch for that light. 'But,' I said, 'you put it out.' 'I know,' he answered. 'It took me some time to find the switch. It was in the caretaker's house next door!'

Interest in the show was so great that it was revived two years later but then, because of the untimely death of Bríd Ní Loinsigh, another actress filled the part of Ansty. Bravely, and with the knowledge of Bríd's outstanding success in the role, Kathleen Barrington took over the part and was acclaimed by the critics for her interpretation. During this run in the Peacock, a play in the Abbey failed to bring the people in. *The Tailor and Ansty* came upstairs and filled the bigger house for two weeks.

I forget how many times the *Tailor* was revived, but on the last occasion my wife Maura played Ansty. P. J. O'Connor always said that he had her in mind for the part when he wrote it. At that time Tomás Mac Anna had brought a young man fresh from Trinity into the Abbey, and it was he who directed the *Tailor* this time. His name was Michael Colgan. He built the show out of the new, like the Tailor making a new suit. Maura's Ansty was busy as a bee, all fuss and fooster, bringing new impetus to the part. The Tailor, because of a gammy leg, was anchored in various positions on the set. In Colgan's direction he was orbited by Ansty, stinging him verbally into action with her acerbic tongue. She was an immediate success. With the bantering and mock-warring conflict between husband and wife, the piece played like a racy tune on an old fiddle.

Again a play in the Abbey was a box office failure, and for a second time the Tailor and his spouse climbed the stairs to the mother house and filled it until a new show was ready.

There was a call from the country again and Maura and I set out on a second *Tailor* tour, this time under the manager-ship of my good friend Ronan Wilmot. We went to Derry and Benburb and south to Macroom, little more than a stone's throw from Garrynapeaka where the Tailor once lived. Coming among people who knew him and Ansty inside out was a bit nerve-racking, but we must have been on the right lines because those who came thoroughly enjoyed the evening's entertainment. They faulted me on one word. What Eric Cross wrote as 'keening' the Tailor would have pro-nounced 'caoining'. I should have known better.

In Macroom on the Saturday night there was only a scattering of people. Ronan Wilmot and John O'Toole, the stage manager, drove out to Gougane near the Tailor's cottage on Sunday. In Cronin's Hotel, after a meal, people who were all dressed up said they were going to Macroom to see their old friend the Tailor. A good omen; interest was growing, and, sure enough, the house was packed that night and the next. Then we drove on to Bantry for more full houses. The old storyteller was being honoured in his own land.

Maura and I made friends with the Tailor's son, Jackie, and his wife, when we visited the Tailor's one-time famous home. The day we were there, Jackie's cow, what his father used to call the dairy herd, was about to calf. She was a friendly creature, as black as a crow, her barrel large, showing that she was near her time. I minded her out of the cabbages for a while, as I used to mind our own cow when I was a child in Carrigeen. I plucked a wide cabbage leaf and she ate it out of my hand. 'You should have been a farmer,' Jackie said, and he promised that if the cow had a bull calf he would call him after me. So it transpired, and when I met Jackie in Cork afterwards, he swore that the calf, which turned out to be a pet, used to answer to my name.

'Éamon,' Jackie said, 'I sold you in Bantry fair last week for ten pounds.'

15

SYNGE AND THE DANDY DOLLS

In Hugh Hunt's time as artistic director at the Abbey one of his first productions was *The Well of the Saints*, Synge's famous play about two beggars. Beggars were very much part of the rural scene when I was young. They weren't all travellers who lived under carts or in caravans, but maybe settled families who once had seen better days. Some people, not blessed with a great share of the world's goods themselves, took them into their homes at night, and they slept on straw on the kitchen floor. Many of the lone men were fine storytellers and in the days before newspapers and radio they brought tales of the Fianna and news of the doings in the big world outside.

Mick and Biddy were a well known pair who came by our house once a month. Mick stood outside and Biddy did the begging. She sometimes sat at the other side of the fire from my mother and drank a cup of tea. When she got something for her beg, she'd bring a cup of tea out to Mick and a slice of hot yella buck cake with butter melting at the top. They were as odd as two left shoes. Mick walked ahead of Biddy, looking back now and then, and calling, 'Come on! Come on! Come on!' She took no notice, but plodded away behind him humming to herself a tuneless air.

Despite their oddness they were never the butt of youthful scorn like poor Nellie Mulcahy, a deranged beggarwoman I saw one time in my travels. Nellie loved bus conductors and spent her few precious pennies on short bus journeys so as to be in the company of the man in the uniform cap, and carrying the money bag and ticket puncher. When she was on foot her unkempt hair blew in the wind; she was a pathetic figure in a black shawl and raggedy skirt. The children taunted her as she made her mad way past them on the road to school.

Synge's two beggars are blind. They live in a world of their own, believing themselves to be beautiful people, a fantasy which is fuelled by cruel villagers. Martin Doul boasts of Mary's beauty, of her bright blue eyes and golden hair, and Mary Doul in her imagination pictures Martin as a handsome prince. They are cured of their blindness by a saint at a holy well, and, in the days before the looking-glass, each sees only the other's ugliness. The stark reality brings bitterness and disappointment.

Their fury knows no bounds. They curse, castigate and attack each other with a passion that burns like fire. In time the cure wears off, and when blindness returns we have followed them in their journey from darkness to light and back to darkness again. We have seen their great rage on discovering that their beauty was only a figment of their fancy.

The angry storms having abated, they sit reconciled in the open air. They revert to their previous pursuit of selling peeled rushes to passers-by. (These rush piths were fried in lard, left to dry, and used as primitive candles.) Sounds are everything when sight is no more. The bleat of a sheep, the rippling of a rill or the swish of a bird's wing catches their attention and is talked about. When stillness comes she reaches for his hand; they smile in contentment and are happy again in the world of the imagination.

I was happy when Hugh Hunt cast me in the part of Martin Doul. Physically I was a little too large of frame to fit my description by Mary Doul when she upbraids me in her anger. But I had a feeling for Synge's language. The lilt of it I had learned from my mother when she recited poetry or was carried away in her flights of picturesque prose. I loved the rise and fall of Synge's speech and I gloried in its delivery. His words are not for measured speaking. They must flow, and at times come off the tongue in a torrent.

Mary Doul was played by Máire Ní Dhomhnaill, no stranger to Synge's language. John Kavanagh was the Saint and Patrick Laffan Timmy the Smith. Alan Barlow's set, of large grey boulders against a treacherous sky, captured the dark, bleak mood of the play. Our opening night was 8 September 1969, and of it Desmond Rushe wrote in the *Irish Independent*: 'There are moments which one always hope-fully waits for in the theatre, but seldom experiences – those rare and terrifying moments which rivet one to one's seat. Hugh Hunt achieves one of them in his brilliant production of J. M. Synge's *The Well of the Saints* at the Abbey Theatre . . . Éamon Kelly plays Martin and Máire Ní Dhomhnaill plays Mary. They are both magnificent. The electrifying moment comes when Martin sees for the first time the woman he has dressed with soft skin, large blue eyes and long golden tresses. His reaction to the reality is a savage eruption of pain. His disillusionment is bitter and total, and he makes the audience share it with him to the full. His playing all through is incisive and superlative, but here he is stunning.'

Seamus Kelly in *The Irish Times* said that Hugh Hunt's direction gave classical treatment to a classical Abbey play.

The Well of the Saints was considered short for a full

night's entertainment and it was the practice then to put on a curtain-raiser with it. This time it was *The Dandy Dolls* by George Fitzmaurice, being produced at the Abbey for the first time and also directed by Hugh Hunt. The experts call Fitzmaurice's plays 'folk fantasies' and *The Dandy Dolls* is wild and weird. It is the story of Roger Carmody, who spends his days making grotesque dolls and his nights raiding the presbytery fowlhouse. The parish priest comes searching for his stolen goose 'with the cuck on her'. Pat Layde, who played Father James, asked me many a time what a 'cuck' was. I didn't know, unless it was a tuft of feathers on the goose's head.

The human characters in the play are Roger, his wife Cauth and their child; Father James, Keerby the priest's clerk and Timmeen Faley. There are also what you would call otherworldly figures like the Grey Man, the Hag of Barna and the Hag's son. The Hag's son seems never to let Roger finish a doll because, as Cauth tells the Grey Man: ' . . . Them dolls are the biggest torment to him in the world. For the Hag's son is against them to the death, and so sure as Roger makes a doll, so sure will the Hag's son, soon or late, come at it, give it a knuckle in the navel, split it in two fair halves, collar the windpipe, and off with him carrying the squeaky-squeak.'

In the end he carries more than the squeaky-squeak, as we hear from Keerby the parish clerk talking to Father James:

Your goose is safe, your reverence, for it's the wonderful thing entirely I now have seen . . . Roger being carried away by the Hag and the Son of the Hag. Riding on two Spanish asses they were, holding him between them by a whisker each, and his whiskers were the length of six feet you'd think, and his nose was the length of six feet you'd think, and his eyes were the size of turnips bulging outside his head. Galloping like the wind they were, through the pass of the Barna mountains, sweeping him along with them, for ever and ever to their woeful den in the heart of the Barna Hills.

Fitzmaurice and Synge were the two sides of the same coin. Synge the outsider who went to the west and to Wicklow and learned the people's language, and Fitzmaurice the insider who wrote in the tongue that was his from the cradle.

Like Synge, Fitzmaurice was a Protestant. He was the son of a parson who married his housekeeper, lost his stipend and turned farmer. George's mother, Winifred O'Connor, was of the old stock, and of course it was from her he heard the language of his plays. Her voice, I would say, echoes through the speeches of his mature women characters. No clucking hens these, but a bevy of songbirds singing it out, arms akimbo, like Maineen in *The Magic Glasses*. The sound of women's voices filled his childhood: his mother talking to the servants, with whom she was all the one, the O'Connor relations coming and going, the women in the neighbouring houses where George, like the young Douglas Hyde in Roscommon, spent much of his time cabin-hunting. Women forever making tapes. As he grew older he moved among and listened to the men, at fair or market, working in his father's fields or talking by the fire at night.

Fitzmaurice's language, like the speech of the people of Duagh in his time, is peppered with Irish words and phrases. 'Boloeeriv' when we first see it in *The Pie-Dish* has an eastern European look about it. Roll it on the tongue and it is nothing more mysterious than the familiar *'Bail Ó Dhia oraibh'* we heard from Mícheál O'Hehir when the ball was thrown in at Croke Park.

The word 'shandanagh' has a more homely appearance and turns out to be the old man in the corner, *an sean-duine*. 'Cleakawn' from *claí*, a small or low fence, is another of the many words which speckle Fitzmaurice's dialogue. Words like 'elaygil', *a laoigh ghil*, a dear one, and 'careshuck', *an chiarseach*, the female blackbird. He captured and caged for us a people's speech in lazy flight from Irish to English. What we hear is what was said, but the artist rearranges.

The people who crowded his youthful days were still very vivid in Fitzmaurice's mind when I knew him but briefly forty years ago. Over a glass of stout he would describe a scene at nightfall in Bedford near Listowel, where he was born: youngsters jeering a servant girl from west Kerry because they had heard she spoke Irish. She took refuge in a house into which they followed her and, cowering in the chimney corner, she told her tormentors that she understood Irish but didn't speak it.

But there was warmth, too, and tolerance. He recalled with some pleasure sitting with his father and the family in a front pew in St Mary's Cathedral in Killarney when their neighbour, Dr Mangan from Bedford, was consecrated Bishop of Kerry.

When I met George Fitzmaurice he was in his eighties and walked slowly, his body thrust forward. As he approached you in the street you found yourself looking into the top of his grey felt hat, the brim so broad that it almost hid his stooped figure. When you spoke to him, and you spoke quietly for he was very shy, he raised his head slowly. Gradually the light of recognition spreading from his eyes lit up his face. Then he smiled and there was a softly spoken greeting. He had a big, round, pleasant face and for his age a fine colour in his cheeks. His eyes were blue and, I think, very large; so was his mouth below a long upper lip. He had a curious habit of moving his mouth in a cud-chewing fashion as he listened. An old raincoat came almost to the ground.

If you met him in O'Connell Street in the afternoon, he was on his way to Woolworth's Café in Henry Street. The lunch rush over, he would take a tray to the self-service counter and retire to a quiet corner to have his meal. I took a curious gent of a literary turn to the top of the stairs one time to see him but I wouldn't for the world have allowed anyone to intrude on his privacy.

You could meet him too at night-time, ambling up Grafton Street. He used to go to Mooney's of Harry Street, an honest-to-God pub then, just across the road from McDaid's. He stood by himself, a lonely figure, the support of the counter keeping him erect. It was here one night that I mentioned his plays and I think this put an end to our brief friendship. I had heard the stories . . . like the pub he hysed himself out of, never to come back, when a country barman asked him, 'Are you the George Fitzmaurice whose plays do be on at the Abbey?'

I wouldn't have drawn down the subject, but that Mícheál Ó hAodha had asked me to try and persuade him to give Radio Éireann permission to broadcast *The County Dressmaker* and *The Magic Glasses*. He turned me down, but gave his permission subsequently.

I think the last place I saw him was in the Winter Gardens, now gone, at the corner of Cuffe Street and the Green. As ever, he was by himself at the far end of the bar. I had gone in there during the interval, the night Brendan Behan's *An Giall* opened at the Damer. He was curious about the sudden influx of thirsty *gaeilgeóirí*, noticing they weren't regulars. I explained. He regretted he hadn't learned some Irish. It was once a major European language, he told me, judging by the placenames, and spoken in Lisbon, Lisieux and Listowel! He pursed his lips and I thought I detected a twinkle in his eye.

'Fine acting in two revivals at the Abbey' is how *The Irish Times* described *The Dandy Dolls* and *The Well of the Saints* when they were brought back in July 1970 for a short run prior to a London transfer for an international theatre festival. We played at the Old Vic and, the gods be praised, as happened on Broadway and on a former visit to the West End, I had a dressing-room to myself.

Cast and crew were put up in the Irish Club in Eaton Square and a bus brought us to and from the theatre. I rarely sleep after the excitement of a first night, and next morning I was up early and went out for a stroll. The uppermost thought in my head was what kind of reception the press would give the plays. I always fear the worst and for that reason made up my mind not to look at the morning papers. As I walked along, what should I see but the buff shade of the *Financial Times* stuck in a railing far from a house entrance. I was tempted to have a look but decided against it. When I was returning, the paper was still there. On an impulse I took it and turned to the arts page.

Anthony Curtis wrote: '*The Dandy Dolls* which we saw last night has a fantastical Celtic cricket-on-the-hearth quality . . . Folk art can be a bit impenetrable if you are not one of the folk and the strange piece, most spiritedly performed, was received with a baffled air by the audience. In England it would have been a Barrie-ish pantomime . . . in Germany it would have all centred on the moment when they nailed the doll down to the table, highly symbolic no doubt, but being Irish it all ends with a bit of good old-fashioned priest bashing.'

Oh well! The Hag of Barna hits Father James once with the broom, which he takes from her and drives the Hag and her son from the house as our Lord drove the moneylenders from the temple.

'No such bafflement,' Anthony Curtis said, 'in *The Well of the Saints.*' And he gave a synopsis of the story. 'As always with Synge,' he continued, 'the dice seem to be loaded for pathos, but there is humour well brought out in the main performances of Éamon Kelly and Máire Ní Dhomhnaill, the peatfire in their bellies burnt brightly in the great slagging matches.' He had praise for the cast, for Hugh Hunt's direction and for the settings of Alan Barlow.

The daily and evening papers displayed various degrees of bafflement at *The Dandy Dolls*, but praised the acting of Éamon Keane, Joan O'Hara, Desmond Cave and Pat Layde.

Commenting on the production of *The Well of the Saints*, Michael Billington in *The Times* complained that 'some rather cumbersome grouping – with too many solid peasant figures planted downstage – obscures some of the most powerful theatrical moments such as the blind peasant's first recognition of the faces around him, after his miraculous healing.'

The press was over from Dublin to cover the event. Gus Smith writing in the *Irish Independent* said that 'Missing from the Old Vic on the first night were the Abbey directors. Strange when you consider that this was an auspicious occasion for the company. One also missed the first night reception for the players at the Irish embassy. Surely this is no way to treat members of Ireland's National Theatre on tour. I regret to have to say that the Abbey Company opened at the Old Vic unheralded and unsung. This will not do!'

In fact, two directors, Gabriel Fallon and Roibeárd Ó Faracháin, came at midweek. We saw them in the bus taking us back to the Irish Club. They were deep in discussion and spoke ne'er a word to any of us.

The Irish Club was fairly central, and when free I renewed

my acquaintance with the city. I went again to the National Gallery, and fed the pigeons in Trafalgar Square. I went too to the Tate Gallery and bought a reproduction of Jack B. Yeats's *Travellers* – two figures met, and in as lively a conversation as that of any Abbey directors, in a multi-coloured landscape in which there were elements of Alan Barlow's setting for *The Well of the Saints*.

I wasn't finished with that play yet. Years later I played the same part in an Irish Theatre Company's touring production. It was directed by Christopher Fitz Simon, and Maura O'Sullivan was a splendid Mary Doul. The curtain-raiser this time was *On Baile's Strand* by W. B. Yeats.

To go out where we came in, George Fitzmaurice, who is gradually gaining recognition outside the shores of Ireland, is now neglected at the Abbey. In my many years there I was in but one of his plays, *The Pie-Dish*. I played the part of an honest potter who, wishing to excel at his art, sells his soul to the devil.

16

DRESSING-ROOM ONE

Dressing-rooms at the Abbey were not allotted according to one's status in a play. There wasn't any one-actor accommodation for those playing leads as in the commercial theatre. In a permanent company like the Abbey had then, permanent actors, once allotted a dressing-room, remained there permanently. It was like a second home to some, and one actor had many of his personal belongings in his desk drawer, including, it was said, the deeds of his house.

In No 1 dressing-room, situated almost under the stage, there were six actors' places on a long bench in front of six mirrors. The mirrors were lit by twenty-one bulbs, three at the sides of each mirror, and all operated by one switch. In the summertime we nearly melted with the heat. There were lamps on the low ceiling too, but the light bulb inside the door was never put in its socket, because when the door was closed it sheared off the bulb – an indication of how well designed the place was. I dressed in No 1 over a period of twenty-eight years. The image of the place is etched in my brain.

In the long bench there were six drawers for the actors' make-up and scripts; in front of it stood six stools, an easy chair and a rack on which to hang costumes; and under it was a stretcher bed on which to lie when exhaustion set in. In the daytime, many is the man slept off the effects of a few pints on it. There was a toilet, two wash-hand basins and a shower. There was hot water in constant supply and very tempting for non-residents.

Pale actors in the company dressed together in Nos 4, 5 and 6. The ladies dressed in Nos 2 and 3. In No 1 there were six players, including myself, all of whom came from the regions. Harry Brogan was the only urbanite. Peadar Lamb and Mícheál Ó Briain, when they talked of home, spoke in mellifluous Connemara Irish. At times when those of us fluent enough joined in, our subterranean chamber took on the air of a tiny gaeltacht.

But there were two other actors present who never spoke directly to each other. Their mutual animosity was manifest. I often opened the door unexpectedly when they were alone to find their voices raised in bitter acrimony. If the walls and mirrors could speak they would reveal the secret of two men passionately in love with one woman. But when cast in a play as long-lost friends, how convincingly they laughed, shook hands and fondly embraced.

Only once did I dress in No 4. That was when Peter O'Toole played in *Waiting for Godot*, and we were all evicted from No 1 to make room for him. He put a gold star on his door, and his name in Irish – Peadar Ó Tuathail. Other stars who came to our theatre from time to time settled in with the regulars.

Democracy in the dressing-rooms had to do with the no-star system at the Abbey, which was always regarded as a writers' theatre. Actors were never mentioned on the posters. The double crown simply said what was on, by whom, what time and how much to get in. All this was stated clearly so that the contents could be gleaned while passing by on a galloping horse. If you stabled your horse and paid your money into the theatre, you could see the actors and read their names in the programme.

I am convinced that I was the first Abbey actor whose name and physiognomy appeared on a poster. During Tomás Mac Anna's second term as artistic director, he asked me to do an evening of storytelling at the Peacock. I became so nervous at the prospect of standing for two hours in front of an audience that had a job been going as barman in a remote tavern in Katmandu I would have taken it.

But one-man shows were becoming popular in the theatre in 1975. Mícheál Mac Liammóir had given the headline in Ireland with his *The Importance of Being Oscar* and *I Must Be Talking to My Friends*. When I got over the shock of being asked, storytelling seemed to me an ideal subject for a one-man show. I had experience of doing longish storytelling spots in concerts, and my part in *The Tailor and Ansty* was in many ways a solo effort.

I got down to throwing some stories together with the theme of emigration, and I called the show *In My Father's Time*. Tomás Mac Anna gave me Michael Colgan to direct it, and, oh lucky me — we got on like two houses on fire. We found that a number of stories told one after the other could sound episodic. There had to be a changing relationship between the pieces, and the links had to be carefully thought out to make seamless the fabric, which we hoped would be colourful and entertaining.

Meabh Browne designed the set, which had as its focal point the fireplace, where storytellers sat since Fionn and Oisín told tales in the king's house in ancient Ireland. Opposite the hearth there was a gable wall, a fly-in roof section overhead, and a freestanding door and window. I was given a say in the selection of the furniture. A *súgán* armchair, two *súgán* chairs, a well worn deal table, a dresser full of shining delph, a foldaway settle bed, a wickerwork turf basket with sods piled high, harness hanging from a peg, and a box on which sat a white enamel bucket of water from which I drank with a mug to punctuate a piece, or to tide me over a round of applause. There was one holy picture to preside over the proceedings.

The mantelpiece had an alarm clock, a tea canister, a candle in a sconce, a small oil lamp and letters from America. Socks and an old shirt hung from a line across the fireplace. There were a kettle, a teapot and another pot suspended from the crane, and downstage a butterbox with a hinged lid which became a seat. Inside it was a regular storehouse and the Tailor, who had one, called it his cornucopia.

Michael Colgan directed me so that I used almost everything on the stage at least once. The armchair was for the long, legendary-type story with the red glow of the fire lighting up my face. Pulling a chair out from the table and standing between them was a gateway. Putting a chair on the table, I sitting at the other end became the driver of an engine pulling a train-load of emigrants out of Killarney station. There were journeys to the turf basket to pile the sods on the fire. There was delph from the dresser, tea from the canister and water from the kettle into the teapot to make the cup that cheers. The table was also a bar or a shop counter to stand behind.

I moved in the set – sat on the chairs, on the butterbox, leaned against the table, sang a song standing by the dresser while putting a reins in the harness bridle – and I tried to do all this with ease and naturalness, without fuss or ado.

Before the performance it would be impossible for me to run the lines, there were so many of them. Instead I topped and tailed the stories, fixed their sequence firmly in my head and thoroughly rehearsed the linking pieces. Opening night came. The heart pounded and I reached out for the hand which guides us mortals in times of stress. The people piled in. They sat on the steps and stood at the back. Tadhg Crowley of the box office said afterwards that for the run we did a hundred and ten per cent business.

The show succeeded beyond all expectations. Because of a misprint in *The Irish Times*, the admission prices at the Peacock were given as 75p and £1000. Seamus Kelly of that paper told his readers that having seen the show it was worth every penny of it. John MacInerney, writing of the evening's entertainment in the *Irish Press*, said, 'Emigration is the focus of many of the tales allowing the storyteller to dovetail accounts of wakes, partings, returns, all night dancing (and how the clergy put the dead hand on all such joy) and matchmaking. Heartbreak and comedy are held in nice balance, and that salty, sly Kerry humour keeps sentimentality alertly at bay.'

So great was the demand that every June for seven years I had a new one-man storytelling show on the stage of the Peacock, all but one directed by Michael Colgan. I toured the country with them. I was in so many places that one man said I must have stopped at every back door in Ireland. One night in the Great Hall of Magee University in Derry the crewman on the curtain told me at the interval that he was going to watch a football match on the box, but that he would be back before the end. He mistimed his return and when I told my last tale I took a bow but the curtain didn't close. I walked into the wings and pressed a button which brought the tabs across. I pressed another button and the curtain opened. I went out and took another bow. I continued to open and close the curtain and take bow after bow until the audience were rocking with laughter and getting to their feet. I received a standing ovation and gave myself as many curtains as Marcel Marceau.

I was in New York in January 1976 as part of Ireland's contribution to America's bicentennial celebrations. Irish talent was well represented. I stepped into an elevator in a Manhattan hotel and found myself blessed among Siobhán McKenna, Marie Kean, Anna Manahan, Aideen O'Kelly and the singer Mary O'Hara. They were in the *Best of Ireland* concert in Carnegie Hall, as were Peter O'Toole, Donal McCann, Niall Tóibín, Niall Buggy, Donal Donnelly and yours truly, in scenes from *Waiting for Godot, Juno and the Paycock, Riders to the Sea, The Playboy of the Western World, Philadelphia, Here I Come!* and *The Loves of Cass McGuire.* All backed up by Geraldine O'Grady, Eily O'Grady, Frank Patterson, Caitriona Yeats, Jesse Owens, Hal Roach, the Clancy Brothers, the Chieftains and the McNiff dancers. An imposing array – a sight to dazzle the eye.

The show was presented to an Irish American audience in the presence of Jim Farley, the Irishman of the century, and in the lobby there was a photography exhibition showing the works of Fergus Bourke.

Of course the whole caboodle was meant to be held in Madison Square Garden, but the New York promotion committee, once formed, split (in the fashion of many Irish movements), and the energy which should have gone into publicity and organisation went into bickering. The Madison Square Garden plan fell through, and we ended up playing to a fairly packed Carnegie Hall, but only for a matinée performance.

Robert C. Roman of the *Irish Echo* declared the show 'an unqualified success . . . a magnificent production'. He said that everyone associated with the afternoon of the best in the cultural and entertainment arts deserved rich praise. News of it spread across the Atlantic and Alfred Paul Berger said in *The Irish Times*: 'The entertainment itself was pervaded with a kind of gentle, endearing innocence too seldom encountered in this hard-bitten age and area. The entire affair was one large Irish Valentine, unabashedly unsophisticated, and the more winning for that. While Siobhán McKenna and Peter O'Toole were most in evidence, the performance was well laced with many more or less recognisable names in all divisions of the arts.'

17

THE CLOTHES

I found that the sense of continuity at the Abbey was a cherished commodity. It hung by a thread of stories told by old actors, parables that went back to the founders of the theatre and to those who practised in it down the years. Many of the tales you could take with a pinch of salt, like the one about a wardrobe seamstress in the old days who was so pious that she wouldn't sew buttons into men's trousers' flies.

The wardrobe was part of the Abbey tradition. When I became a member there was a great stock of costumes used in the theatre's repertoire of native plays. Each director selected garments from this collection for his new production. The store contained costumes designed by the artist Seán Keating for a production of *The Playboy of the Western World* in the 1940s. There were items which must have come from Connemara or the Aran Islands, for their handiwork had all the crude honesty of a country tailor.

From his hand came grey and brown *bréidín* (tweed) coats, collared waistcoats, *báiníns*, trousers and knee breeches for the men. There were red flannel skirts for the women. An assortment of aprons and brown-and-fawn paisley shawls with tassels. These last could have walked off the oil painting by Grace Henry of three shawled Connemara women bunched together on a hill. Among all these items there was a gent's tweed coat, faded and foxy and built in the cutaway fashion of the last century. It came to just above the knees and had large pocket flaps. It was much the worse for wear, with frayed edges and the padding protruding from a tear in the left shoulder. I wore it many times and got so fond of it that I became jealous if I saw it on another actor's back.

It fitted as if it was made for me, and with a neckcloth, knee breeches and long grey homemade stockings, the outfit on me looked the real goat's toe in any turn of the century native play; even more so if topped with a battered, greenish, floppy felt hat and supported by a pair of boots so old and pliable they could have first been worn by Barry Fitzgerald. It was my costume in the character of Old Mahon in *The Playboy of the Western World* and Scots people got an eyeful of it when we took the play to the Edinburgh Festival. The Irish collection, as I'll name those old costumes, was part of the Abbey's continuity.

It was in Hugh Hunt's time as artistic director that a lady from Manchester took over as wardrobe mistress for a while. She must have been flabbergasted at the collection of Aran Islands and Connemara drapery, the likes of which she'd have never seen in the illustrations in her theatre costume textbooks. Anyway she got rid of the whole motley caboodle. What happened to my tweed coat I do not know.

I would have liked if 'the clothes', as Harry Brogan always called the costumes, went to the St Vincent de Paul. And it could be so, for one day I am almost certain I saw my foxy coat on the back of a poor man fingering the keys of a decrepit concertina in Talbot Street. A dark green hat with a scattering of coppers inside lay by his ancient boots. If the coat was mine it was still in show business.

It may be only a fancy, but my feeling is that the old Abbey went out the door with those costumes. The permanent company to all intents and purposes is gone and there are new faces before the footlights.

18

WHITE-KNUCKLE FLIGHTS

In mid-February of 1976 I was haring across the Atlantic again, on my way to Newfoundland to contribute to the Canadian Association for Irish Studies seminar in the University of St John's. Author Bryan MacMahon, playwright M. J. Molloy, the folklorist Kevin Danaher and many more were on the team from Ireland.

Bryan spoke about Peig Sayers and the vernacular of the storyteller, M. J. Molloy on the making of folk plays and Kevin Danaher on the customs and lore of the countryside. There were readings by the poet Thomas Kinsella, and Eileen O'Casey talked about her husband, Seán.

Bryan and I enjoyed that trip to Newfoundland and rejoiced in the company of the other contributors and the many new friends we made there. We relaxed when our work was over. As we were talking quietly one night in a crowded room, and thinking back to the time when we first met playing in the local drama group twenty-five years before, Bryan said, with an air of pride, 'Ned, we've come a long way.' 'Yes,' I answered, 'only three thousand miles.' He lowered his left eyelid and said, 'amparan', a Listowel word implying derision. Dineen defines 'amparach' as a helpless human condition of being bloated with swelling. The familiar expression in strange surroundings made us laugh heartily.

Talking about our own contributions to the seminar, Bryan said that during my show, *In My Father's Time*, his attention was drawn to a group of Eskimos, young men and women who were students at the university, and he wondered how on earth would they respond to the indigenous humour of my stories. At first some were bewildered while others enjoyed the telling, but then some throwaway line or gesture must have reminded them of the idiosyncrasies of an old man in their own village, because they broke into almost uncontrollable laughter. They fell silent and their eyes glistened when death was mentioned, or the pain of parting during the emigration from Ireland in the 1920s.

Many of the Irish fishermen from the Cork and Waterford coasts who sailed, in the last century, to the rich fishing grounds of *Talamh an Éisc* settled in and around St John's. In the streets and in the shops there is a noticeable Irish lilt to the people's speech. At a television station I could have sworn I heard one crewman say to another, 'Are 'ou all right there now, boy?' The taxi drivers' accents sounded Irish, slightly diluted, and Aidan O'Hara, who worked for a long time in Newfoundland, told me that Irish words linger on in everyday speech.

I was in a house one Sunday where worshippers had gathered after Mass. As at home, there was a cup of tea going, and one lady was asked to stay on for a mouthful. 'Oh no,' she said, 'I am in a hurry. There's a *slua* at home waiting for me.' She had a large family depending on her attention. *Slua*, of course, is the Irish word for a crowd.

Irish surnames like Tobin and Brennan gaze down from the fascia boards of shop fronts. The native sense of the ridiculous is akin to our own. A man in a car running eastwards to the sea stopped and asked a Newfoundlander working in a field, 'Is this the road to Ireland?' ''Tis,' the farmer replied, 'but you'd want to be careful. 'Tis flooded beyond the lighthouse!'

There was an arrangement with the university whereby we visitors stayed with Irish families. I was the guest of Dr Michael Mangan and his wife, who is also a doctor. Michael, who hails from Galway, owned racehorses in Ireland at that time, and there was one very famous animal of his called Monksfield, small and compact, which made a great name for himself. When I came home I saw him on TV win hands down at Cheltenham.

Michael had a bar down in the cellar. This speakeasy, as he called it, is a feature of many houses in the States too. There's a counter complete with flap and a little door to get in. Shelves of bottles, many of them of Irish origin, line the back wall. There's a fridge for the beer and the place is decorated with Guinness and whiskey signs brought over from Ireland. A few tables, easy chairs and a high stool or two. A cosy place for a quiet drink after a hard day. Many is the after dinner-hour I sat outside the bar, Michael inside, as we talked into the night, and the talk was always of home.

As part of an educational scheme St John's University sent me out to speak to dramatic societies throughout the province of Newfoundland. I was to conduct a workshop one evening and put on my own storytelling show the next. My first stop was Labrador. The February weather was vile. Snowflakes flew thick and fast past the window of the plane. By air seems to be the only way of getting about, and the planes fly in the most atrocious weather. In the jolting and buffeting in the storm, passengers hold on desperately to their seats, grasping the armrests in such a tight grip that these journeys are known as 'white-knuckle flights'.

My heart came up into my mouth one time as the plane seemed to stop. Outside the window was white with driving snow, and as there was little difference between the bumping in the sky and that experienced when landing, I thought we were still in the air. I held my breath, waiting for the plane to fall; but the French-English announcement of the bilingual Canadian steward proclaimed that we had landed.

Wahbush is the airport for Labrador. The two places, some miles apart, are known as the twin cities, but in actual fact they are no bigger than a small Munster town, and came into being because of the discovery of large deposits of iron ore. When the snowploughs clear the runways, the channel made looks as if a knife had cut through the icing of a cake with banks of snow at either side. The streets are the same, and so cold, thirty degrees below, that if taxis turn off their engines they can't start them again. It is easy to find a taxi rank. There's a cloud of exhaust smoke over it. Motorists have a heater inside the car and another in the engine.

When the vehicle is parked at home or at work there is a long flex to the heater which is plugged into the electricity. Otherwise the moisture would freeze in the door locks and the oil would solidify in the engine. The streets are always frozen, and a car couldn't negotiate a sharp rise without chains wound round the tyres.

Wahbush and Labrador are three hundred miles inland and eighteen hundred feet over sea level. Because of the altitude, the air is thin and a newcomer falls asleep on his feet. A man brought me out to see the open mining and three times I fell asleep in the car. Trains, miles long, are travelling night and day, bringing iron ore to the coast for export. I was told that the trains were driverless, operated by electricity, but that could have been a Newfoundlander pulling my leg. What took my fancy, though, were the massive tractors with scoops in front for shifting the iron ore. To give an idea of their size, my picture was taken beside one and my head just came up to the axle of the wheel.

The space in which I did my storytelling show in Labrador was a games centre and far too large. It lacked the intimacy of a theatre. A sprinkling of Irish in the audience helped the reaction and forged a bond across the footlights. The workshop the evening before was full of interest for me as John B. Keane's *Sive* was the next play the society was to perform. The Irish, some from home and some from St John's, had plenty of work in the iron ore industry. There were Northern Irish there too, and the city of Wahbush boasted an Orange and a Hibernian hall. Protestants and Catholics tended to drift into separate communities when they settled in the New-foundland countryside, and the weathercock or cross on the church spires revealed their identities.

In the twin cities only Wahbush had a hotel, where I stayed. My bedroom window overlooked what must have been a playing field in the summer, because the top of a soccer goal-post showed a few inches above the snow. Disposable paper slippers (mine fitted) were provided for one's journeys to the bathroom, and the heat was blown in, which reminded me of a night spent years before in a motel in Wilmington, Delaware. Thank God there was a great log fire in the dining-room.

From Labrador I flew to Gander. As we came in to land, a large bird (in Gander of all places) crashed into the windscreen of the plane and cracked the glass. It could have been serious had the screen been breached. Those flying on to St John's had to take another plane.

I enjoyed doing my own show in Gander, but the work-shops, sometimes two a day, became slightly arduous, though the children in the schools were delightful and entered with gusto into my near insane projects. I told a story, which a volunteer among them retold, and then they acted it out on the floor. They improvised with imagination and assumed the characters of the little red hen, the cat and the mouse of the narrative.

The enchanted cake, when it was about to be eaten, ran away, followed by the cat and the mouse and the little red hen. In the chase they were joined by a crumply horned cow and a saddlebacked sow. They passed through a meadow full of mowers, by a barn full of threshers and a riverside full of washerwomen, all of whom joined in the chase. A sly old fox cornered the cake and they all sat around in a circle and had a feast.

They improvised the king's orchard where his son guarded the apples from the great eagle with the feathers of gold, whose eyes were as big as the moon and as bright as the sun. They simulated an aeroplane, complete with pilots ('This is your captain speaking') and hostesses ('Fasten your seat-belts, please') and passengers holding on to their seats in a white-knuckle flight over Newfoundland. They impersonated the storm and the noise of the engines and regretted when I left and took my daftness with me.

My next stop was Cornerbrook where I met the son of novelist Maurice Walsh. He had chains around his tyres as he drove me over icy roads to a secondary school where they were preparing for a performance of Synge's *Riders to the Sea*. In giving them the background to the play, I remembered my holiday in Inis Meáin and my visit to Ceata Bheag's house, where Synge stayed when he came to live in the Aran Islands. Ceata Bheag was busy at her housework when a party of us arrived. She excused herself, went into the room, and came back with a stylish apron and a shoulder shawl. She greeted each person individually in Connacht

Irish, which, because of the island's proximity to Clare, had a little of the Munster music. We couldn't have been received more graciously by the Queen of England. She sat on a fireside chair and, like a queen, held court.

I hoped that the actress playing the part of Maurya in *Riders to the Sea* might take her as a model. I told the students about life on the island and about the sea on which the people depended for a living. The ocean was their orchard, their meadow and their garden.

The students read their parts and, in spite of their Canadian-American accents, the magic of the words came through. They laughed at me at first when I tried to teach them the lament – the *caoineadh* – of the women as Bartley's drowned body is brought back on a door from the sea. Finally they got the lilt of it. It sounded great, and the sorrowing mother's closing speech would soften the heart in a stone:

> It isn't that I haven't prayed for you, Bartley, to the
> Almighty God. It isn't that I haven't said prayers in the
> dark night till you wouldn't know what I'd be saying;
> but it's a great rest I'll have now, and it's time surely.

When I came back to St John's I wrote a report on my activities – the limbers, the improvisations, the rehearsals, all the phases of the work I had done – and gave it to Mr D. Ferry of the Arts and Culture Centre. He was so pleased with the account that the ghost walked immediately and I got the bread, always a fitting culmination to a bout of hard work. My next stop would be New York. Ted Auletta had arranged with me to take part in a concert presented by Carmel Quinn in Carnegie Hall on 6 March.

The morning came for me to leave Newfoundland. It had

snowed so heavily the night before that Michael Mangan had to give me his wellingtons to walk from the house to the taxi. I have them still. Many people from the province go down to New York on day trips, and Dr and Mrs Mangan told me that when a man comes to immigration he holds up his passport and says, 'I'm only down for de day.' I did just that and it worked. No delay, I was waved through.

Waiting in my dressing-room in Carnegie Hall on the night of the show, I was surprised to hear over the tannoy an artist on stage telling one of my stories. I had many imitators at home but I didn't think the malady had spread across the Atlantic. Imitation, it is said, is a form of flattery. Flattery I could have done without that night, because the story he was telling was on my list for the concert and I had to rack my brains for another and rehearse it in the little time I had left. I went on and couldn't have wished for a better reception.

After the show I met Billy Nolan, a son of Liselton, and a diplomat attached to the Irish Consulate in New York. I shall not forget his kindness to me. For safety's sake I had mailed home most of the fee I had earned in Newfoundland, leaving myself with the plane fare and spending money in New York. By a miscalculation I had left myself short and was unable to afford my next meal. Billy must have sensed my predicament. He stood me a dinner in a Russian restaurant nearby. The waiter, when I told him I was a vegetarian, prepared a gorgeous meal for me, so unlike another American waiter who, when I said I didn't eat meat, wanted to know if I was some kind of nut.

I had to go back to Carnegie Hall a few times before I got my fee from Ted Auletta. Some Americans hate parting with money. When I got the dollars I had enough to tide me over to my next engagement, which was with the Irish American Cultural Institute. This was Eoin McKiernan's Irish Fortnight, a tour of United States universities in the days around St Patrick's Day.

Eoin had sent me the schedule and a hundred dollars. I'd have no expenses on the road, he assured me. I had my air tickets, which he enclosed, and I would be met at the airport at each venue and put up in an Irish American homestead. The majority of the houses I visited were quite palatial, with swimming pools and as many bathrooms as we had bedrooms at home. The owners were the successful Irish, the grandchildren and great-grandchildren of penniless emigrants. They were rich, friendly, hospitable to a fault, and every mother's son and daughter of them as handsome as the famous Kennedy family.

I criss-crossed America, starting in Pittsburgh, where I stayed with Arthur Fedel, a scion of France whose Irish connection was that he had been to Trinity College – on a postwar GI scholarship. In after years he researched the work of writer Francis MacManus for his PhD. Arthur walked with me to the university, where I gave my first show on the night of 10 March. He had a sheaf of fliers advertising the events of the coming fortnight. He handed them out to passers-by, good-humouredly extolling the virtues of what was on offer. To a rather reluctant young lady he said, 'You must be Irish. You have red hair. Take one!' She did.

Eoin McKiernan always had at least fourteen contributors in the air in the daytime, so that there was an event taking place simultaneously in that number of universities that night. Sometimes, arriving at a venue in the early morning, I would meet another contributor setting out. Men half my age were complaining that the gruelling schedule was getting them down.

We had on our list Ruaidhrí de Valera, Desmond Guinness, Diarmuid Ó Muirithe, Michael Hartnett, Aidan O'Hara, Nicholas Furlong, Margaret MacCurtain and many more. I did my show at twelve centres in fourteen days, from Omaha, Nebraska, to Holyoke, Mass., from Albany to San Antonio in Texas, and places in between. Inside two weeks I had experienced the icy cold of Labrador and the heat of old king sol splitting the stones in Texas.

Monsignor Michael McManus was my host in San Antonio. The hundred dollars Eoin McKiernan had given me at the outset was gone and I was on my uppers again. The good monsignor must have seen this in my eyes because, on shaking hands with me as I was going, he left a fifty-dollar bill in my palm.

Dr Rona Fields introduced me to the audience when I spoke at Clark University in Worcester, Mass. Jewish, with red hair and blue eyes, she gloried in that part of her heritage that was Irish. Rochester, Minnesota, brought me to the house of my brother-in-law, Dr Michael O'Sullivan, and his wife Margaret. Familiar faces and talk of home helped me to relax, and after a few beers Michael and I went native and sang 'The Valley of Knockanure'. The lecture room in Rochester stands out in my mind because of the fact that nearly everyone in the audience had a camera or a tape recorder. I was no more than settled in when the lights began to flash and microphones like snakes' heads rose out of the dark and crept towards the platform.

My last engagement was at Fordham University, Lincoln Centre, New York. I stayed with my dear friends Jack and Jeanie Cronin in Yonkers. Next morning I had my last letter from Eoin McKiernan, in English this time. He generally wrote in Irish. He thanked me for my contribution to the Irish American Cultural Institute's Fortnight. 'You have done beautifully,' he rounded off. 'You have demonstrated a great art, and charmed great audiences. You have been a wonderful ambassador for Ireland.'

He enclosed my fee. Jack, Jeanie and I went out for a meal and a few drinks that evening. Tomorrow I would board the Aer Lingus skyship — St Brendan or St Bridget — and hyse home to Ireland.

19

STORY THEATRE

Lelia Doolan was artistic director at the Abbey after Alan Simpson but her term of office ended abruptly. I thought she was treated harshly. At actors' meetings a number of the male members – the old stagers, some of them in the Abbey for twenty-five years – were less than gentlemanly to her. During her stay Tomás Mac Anna came up with an idea for story theatre in Irish at the Peacock, with which she readily agreed. It was to be called *Scéal Scéalaí – Story Storyteller*. Tomás asked me to join him in dramatising some of my stories for the stage, and together we put on paper an evening's entertainment, not unlike the Hail Mary, the first part of which was made by the Angel Gabriel and the Church made the last.

Tomás assembled a cast and we went into rehearsal. As well as the dramatised folktales, we had music, mime, song and dance. The setting was of batik hangings by Bernadette Madden, and the basic costumes were of the same material. In one of my stories about the fairy host – 'The Changeling', it was called – infrared light was used, and on the darkened stage white and light colours showed up dazzlingly bright and gave an otherworldly atmosphere to the scene.

Tomás organised a small orchestra which included Seosamh MacCionnaith, Seán Ó Duibhir, Mary Bergin and Mary's sister Antoinette. Father Pat Ahern of Siamsa Tíre in Tralee directed the music and song and taught the actors to dance to an Irish tune. Tomás Mac Anna was the overall director and, because of his long association with panto-mimes in Irish at the Abbey, he had a distinct flair for this type of theatre. His was a rare talent for positioning, grouping and moving actors on stage.

The storyteller, sitting at the side, opened the tale and, as his characters materialised, the actors, as it were, leaped from his imagination and the story became alive. When it was not feasible, visually, to move the story ahead, the storyteller took over momentarily, in much the same way as a narrator in a radio play.

My contributions were mostly in the first half, interspersed with dance and song. We had a giant and a horse, not the pantomime type but the traditional wren boys' animal which roams the streets of Dingle on St Stephen's Day.

It was a happy show and went down well. It was described as 'exquisite', 'spectacular' and 'delicious' by the critics. Desmond Rush wrote in the *Independent*: 'The folklore and folkmusic blend superlatively well, which elevates *Scéal Scéalaí* above any other entertainment of its kind I have seen in the Abbey or the Peacock.' Because Tomás Mac Anna was unable to accompany us, I as co-author of *Scéal Scéalaí* was made director of our two gaeltacht tours. We played first in the Taibhdhearc in Galway. I remember when the run was over and the actors were sitting in the lounge of the Ardilaun House Hotel, where we were staying, when news of Bloody Sunday in Derry came on television.

The sight of Father Edward Daly with his white handkerchief, pleading for a safe passage for the wounded, filled our hearts at once with shock and admiration. When the full tally of those killed by the military became known, anti-British feeling ran high in Galway and throughout the country.

Our next show was in Carraroe in west Galway the following night. We arrived there in the morning and were busy setting up the stage when a group of people arrived and I was told in meticulous Irish that because of the bloodshed in Derry, if the show went ahead that night history would be made in Carraroe. Despite the sweetness of the speech there was no doubting the threat their words carried.

I rang Dublin. The Abbey wanted me to go ahead with the show. They were at a safe distance. I was on the spot and didn't fancy trouble. I discussed the matter with Tadhg Crowley the tour manager and the actors, and we decided to postpone the show for one night as a mark of sympathy with the relatives of the dead in Derry. That night at the time of the show there was Mass in the local church, and the priest invited the actors to intone prayers, from a script which he had given them, for the repose of the souls of the dead, for the comfort of the living and for the forgiveness of those who perpetrated such a heinous crime. He wanted me to pray that God would put Paisley *ar bhóthar a leasa* (on the road of rectitude). I didn't feel like doing so, and made an excuse to get out of it.

Next morning Peadar Lamb and I, with a broadcasting unit hired in Galway, went around the district publicising the fact that the postponed show would be held that night. We turned up the volume to reach houses far in from the public road. People crowded to the doors to listen, and animals in the fields stopped their grazing and wandered in our direction, attracted by the augmented sound of music and speech, something they didn't hear every day.

The show was a success that night in Carraroe and the night after in Spiddal. Our next stop was in Inis Mór in the Aran Islands. The settings, lights, costumes, props and crew went in by boat. Tadhg Crowley the touring manager and the actors travelled by Aer Aran. I remember actor Clive Geraghty gave his plane seat to Finnola Eustace who was our stage manager. There was a bumpy landing on the grass runway on the island.

When we got settled up in our lodgings – I slept in the presbytery in a bed reserved for the bishop when he visited his island parish – we got down to setting the scene in the local hall. The ESB didn't go to Aran then and our electric power was from an oil-driven generator. The stress must have been too much for the engine because the power failed half an hour before the show. I had visions of scouring the island for candles and oil lamps which would have been a poor substitute for the lighting effects devised by Tomás Mac Anna and Mick Doyle.

Mick worked like the trooper he was on the generator, and by reducing the load to suit the machine's capacity, with only a little time to spare before the afternoon show the lights came on to a mighty cheer.

Schoolchildren made up most of our first audience, and it was heart-warming to see their young faces in the front rows all aglow at the splash of colour, at the music, the dance and the sight of the giant and the pantomime horse. For these children it was their first experience of a travelling show and their reaction was different from their mainland cousins. When the final curtain came down there was no applause. We bowed a second time but there was no putting together of hands. But the children weren't disappointed. From their laughing faces and their animated conversation there was no mistaking their happiness.

Applause wasn't stinted at the night's performance, and when it ended the audience remained in the hall. In a while's time musicians appeared, the seats were pushed back and the local people took to the floor in a set dance. I have never heard dance music played so fast, or with such vigour, and the sound of heel and toe on the boarded floor nearly lifted the roof. We actors joined in the merriment, as our hosts tapped out a welcome to us. Their merry feet seemed to beat out an appreciation of what they had seen on stage.

Next day Fergus Bourke took the cast in costume out on the rocks to take some pictures. The ladies were posing in a group when two young men of Aran came by on tractors one behind the other. They were attracted by the loveliness of the scene, and looked in that direction. To savour the view all the more the man in front stopped his vehicle suddenly, and the man behind, not noticing, ran into him. They were going slowly and not much damage was caused by a shapely leg turning a head.

In Tourmakeady we played in the convent. It was a boarding school, and in the afternoon we gave a performance for the girl students. There was a meal for us in the convent refectory afterwards. That night the local people piled in, and the nuns who hadn't seen the afternoon show came. Backstage opened on to a wide landing with a stairway leading to the college dormitory. The young ladies, taking advantage of the nuns' being at the show, climbed out of bed, and in their dressing gowns sat on the steps like angels draped on a celestial stairway. Bryan Murray, Clive Geraghty and the young actors were the object of their interest.

We stayed in Belmullet when we played in Aughleam, the west Mayo gaeltacht by Blacksod Bay. When I looked out the window in Belmullet the first morning the streets were crowded; lots of cars parked and moving about. At breakfast I enquired if there was a fair or market being held, and I was told that it was dole day. Out walking later, I saw country people buying vegetables in the shops. I thought this odd while acres of their land lay fallow.

Even though Aughleam was a gaeltacht, we got the impression from various things that were said in Belmullet that there might not be too great a welcome from the powers-that-be for a show in Irish. We wondered what kind of reception we were going to get.

We arrived in Aghleam next morning to find that the posters advertising the show lay unopened in the presbytery. Better late than never, so we distributed them then and got a broadcasting unit to publicise the evening's entertainment throughout the district and into Belmullet. We didn't meet the parish priest; the curate opened the hall for us. He was a pale-faced, puffy-cheeked man with an inordinate amount of white in his eye. His black hat sat squarely on his head and his countenance ne'er broke into a smile when he greeted us.

There was no seating in the hall, a fact that hadn't been made known to our touring manager when the place was rented. The curate's solution was that those who came could stand. Tadhg Crowley and myself said that on no account would we expect an audience to stay on their feet for two hours. He told us that others who had rented the hall had played to a standing audience, and if it was good enough for them it was good enough for us.

That remark got our dander up, and without putting a tooth in it, we told him that it wasn't good enough for us. Tadhg went into the convent in Belmullet and got two lorry-loads of chairs from the school. God bless the nuns! Now, by placing the loose stools from around the walls of the hall at the front, we had enough seating for the big crowd that came. That night, performance-wise, the show turned out to be one of the best of the tour.

Afterwards the chairs had to be loaded on the transport to take them back to the convent in Belmullet. This, together with striking the set and putting our props and costumes and furniture on the bus, took time, and the curate was furious at the delay. He wanted to lock the hall. 'Mr Keane' he called me as he pulled out the plug of the electric fire where Mícheál Ó Briain was drying his cap in the dressing-room. He ordered us out from backstage.

Tadhg Crowley always made a point of paying the owner of the hall when the show was over. In this case, because of the unfriendliness of the curate, he decided to let him wait. 'There'll be a cheque in the post for you,' he said to him.

Outside the darkened hall there were flashes of lightning, and the roll of approaching thunder. As we piled into the bus all heaven broke loose overhead. I was last on the entry line, and was about to place my hand on the door handle when a flash of lightning ricocheted off it, and little stars danced on the chromium plating. Soon the rain and the hailstones pelted down on the roof of the bus, and almost drowned out the music and song as we sped towards Belmullet.

Next morning our journey was north to Gweedore, where it was a pleasure to play in a fully equipped little theatre.

Our second gaeltacht tour a year later brought us south of the line from Dublin to Galway. The entire cast and crew travelled by bus, the back portion of which had been converted to take the scenery, lighting, costume and props. On our way to a one-night stand in Reenroe Hotel in Ballinskelligs we stopped by the graveyard in Spunkane, near Waterville, where the well known actress Bríd Ní Loinsigh is buried. Those of us who had worked with her, Peadar Lamb, Mícheál Ó Briain, Joan O'Hara, Máire Ní Ghráinne and myself, went in and dropped a prayer pebble on her grave. The younger people remained on the bus. They said they had never heard of her. Impermanent, indeed, is the actor's craft.

We all stayed in Reenroe Hotel. We dressed where we slept, and walked downstairs ready to go on stage, which was in the hotel dining-room. Not an ideal place. We found that the carpets and window drapes deadened the sound a little. In the bar later a local man said to me that song, dance, music and story were all very fine, but he would have preferred a straight drama. Why didn't we bring Mícheál Mac Liammóir's *Diarmuid agus Gráinne*? I told him that the Abbey had toured the gaeltacht areas a few years earlier with an Irish version of *The Colleen Bawn*, and that *Scéal Scealaí* was another aspect of the theatre people might like to see.

'Have another pint,' he said, 'and bring a play the next time.'

We visited Cork, Listowel, Ventry and Coolea, where I met many Irish-speaking friends. This gaeltacht is just over the hill from where I was born. I was in my element here, being the only Munster person in the cast. Kay Kent of *The Irish Times* visited us and stayed with the company till we reached our next stop, which was Ballingeary.

'Going round with the Abbey Company from hall to hall,' she wrote, 'one realises that this village to village touring is every bit as important a part of the National Theatre's work as is playing to its regular audiences in Dublin.'

The Ballingeary hall where we played housed Coláiste na Mumhan (Munster College) where people went to learn Irish in the early days of the Gaelic League. Indeed I had been there thirty years ago on the same errand. A woman in a shop in the village told Kay Kent that I had stayed in her house then. The poster in the window advertising our show had my name underlined in red.

I remembered that summer of long ago and the evenings spent *céilí* dancing in the hall. Like nearly all the young men who go to an Irish summer course, I fell in love, and we climbed the mountain above Gougane Barra lake together. We strayed the river banks along and talked love in Irish that didn't as yet have the fluency to match the passion of the hour.

While in Ballingeary with the show, the cast stayed in Gougane Barra Hotel hard by the Tailor's cottage and next door to Dinny Cronin's house. Both houses belonged to the Cronin brothers and sat at the edge of the lake shore. In the daytime, rambles by the lake, browsing on the pilgrimage island and strolling in the new forest full of wild life were treats for all of us, but more so for those brought up in the city. Tommy Rogers, a crewman who had never been out of Dublin except for a visit to the Isle of Man, had thought such wonderful scenery didn't exist in Ireland.

Mrs Cronin the hotel proprietress endeared herself to all with her friendliness and wonderful cooking. The beating of her omelette I haven't tasted at home or abroad. She was a gentle lady and grew in our visitors' estimation when I told them that her brother was a cardinal in America. There was a party for us on the last night. Neighbours came in and one young lady sang the beautiful Munster song, '*An Binsín Luachra*' ('The Bench of Rushes'). Young local performers gave a *combrá beirte* (a comic conversation in Irish) which had won them a prize at the Irish language festival in Dublin. We had music, step-dancing and stories.

We heard of the monster (*ollaphiast*) which grew so big in the lake in olden times that fish were no longer left to appease its appetite, so it began to eat the monks. The abbot put a curse on it and the giant reptile-like creature, activated by a fierce fire raging in its bowels, worked its way out of the lake and eastwards through Inchageela to Cork harbour. The top lakewater followed in its wake and so the River Lee was formed. A tall tale as old as Methuselah. But the night's entertainment had all the basic ingredients of the show we were doing on the stage every evening.

20

THE EAGLE FLIES OUT
ON THE WREN'S BACK

Later in 1976, and to make a further Irish contribution to the celebrations of the American bicentennial year, the Abbey Theatre was invited to bring a play to the Brooklyn Academy of Music in New York. The tour was also to take in a number of cities in New England. American Actors' Equity stipulates that a visiting company must bring two shows. This would have been a heavy burden on the theatre's resources, so the management of the Abbey hit on the idea of making my storytelling evening the second leg of the tour.

When I was in New York for the Eoin McKiernan Irish Fortnight in March, I put on *In My Father's Time* at the Irish Centre for Harvey Lichtenstein, head of the Brooklyn Academy, to see. He approved, and at the end of November for the third time that year I crossed the Atlantic. Michael Colgan, who directed the show and managed my Irish tour, was with me on the flight, as was the Abbey Company with Cyril Cusack, Siobhan McKenna, Angela Newman and John Kavanagh, to name but a few, who were playing in *The Plough and the Stars*.

The availability of my show and its inexpensive outlay made the tour possible. It was a reversal of the old folktale, I joked with Michael – the eagle was flying out on the wren's back. My set, stage furniture, props and costume had gone on to New York by surface some time before.

The Plough and the Stars was put on in the large auditorium of the Brooklyn Academy and my show in the smaller Lepercq space upstairs. The auditorium of the Lepercq sloped up from the stage edge, and a member of the audience, if he so wished, could walk on to the acting area.

At the interval on the first night this is exactly what Irish people did. They came and sat on the chairs, on the settle, and 'warmed' themselves to the very realistic Leslie Scott fire in my cottage kitchen. They examined and touched everything – artefacts which reminded them of home. Michael Colgan, who came back to the stage to supervise the setting for part two, found them walking away with sods from the turf basket. One woman was putting a *caorán* (fragment of a sod) into her handbag. Michael remonstrated with her. She said that another lady had gone off with a full sod, and why was he making an exception of her? For the rest of the run a crewman had to stand guard, or items irreplaceable in New York would have gone to decorate the sideboards of Irish American homes in Yonkers and Queens. But it was heartwarming that the Irish had turned up in such numbers and I was kept busy afterwards autographing my programme. This was a stylish affair with notes by the folklorist Dr Seán Ó Súilleabháin and writer Con Houlihan.

Michael Colgan and I knew of the tradition whereby anyone with a show opening in New York stayed in that literary and theatrical sanctum, the Hotel Algonquin. I remember visiting it when Brian Friel stayed there during the run of *Philadelphia, Here I Come!* The hotel was a cut above the common and a necktie and jacket were *de rigueur* in the lobby, the restaurant and the bar. But the porter was known, for a consideration, to fetch a tie and jacket from his cubicle if one came unprepared. Michael and I booked in there before opening night. We were welcome from the outset. I knew the desk clerk, who used to work in the Excelsior Hotel in 82nd Street when I was in New York in 1966. He saw to it that we were seen after.

I was the first to get a cab. I was called from the end of the line and walked past potentates from Texas with ten-gallon hats to the summons of 'Mr Kelly, your cab!' The doorman who hailed me was my first cousin Pat Curtin. He was the son of Tim Curtin from Muingnamunane, near Castleisland, who was married to my Aunt Margaret in Queens.

The Algonquin at that time boasted one of the biggest tomcats I had ever seen. This marmalade monster sat on his bottom in the middle of the lobby and mewed to clients whom he perceived to be cat lovers. I patted him on the head and got a love-bite that nearly took a finger away. The lobby had a newspaper and magazine stand. The owner, a friendly New Yorker, remembered the Irish who had stayed in the hotel. He talked of Jack McGowran and he told me what Brendan Behan said to the lady in the fur coat — a remark positively refreshing if unprintable.

This good man (Pat Curtin must have had him primed) laid aside for me the papers that carried reviews of the show after opening night. I did well, but one reviewer claimed that for a while, until he got used to it, my Kerry brogue had him guessing. The same complaint had been made about the Dublin accent in *The Plough and the Stars*, although Sean Cronin, writing from New York in *The Irish Times*, said the night he was at *In My Father's Time*, the reaction of the audience to my stories suggested that there was no language barrier.

The first paper the magazine man in the lobby gave me was *Newsday*, and Amei Wallach said that '*In My Father's Time*, which is devised and written by Éamon Kelly and nicely directed by Michael Colgan, deals with another side of Ireland from that dealt with in the Abbey Company's first offering, Seán O'Casey's *The Plough and the Stars*. In contrast to the fierce fighting and carousing of Dubliners depicted by O'Casey, Kelly is telling of a more gentle people in rural Ireland and their less belligerent pleasures . . . He elicits laughter while evoking the past.'

Mel Gussow of the *New York Times* remembered me from *Philadelphia, Here I Come!* some ten years earlier, and pictured me thus: 'with his hat sitting squarely on his head, his baggy suit looking freshly crumpled, and wearing the bemused look of an aging leprechaun, he begins to populate the stage with fathers and mothers, stonemasons and parish priests, beautiful young women and anxious young men. *In My Father's Time* almost becomes a one-man Irish approximation of *Under Milk Wood*. In the end this is an enveloping evening. We are drawn into Mr Kelly's world — folksy, amiably far-fetched and with a touch of vinegar.'

Patricia O'Haire of the *New York Daily News* headed her piece with 'An Emerald Darlin' of a Storyteller' (you'd have to go to the States to get that one) and ended by saying, 'His theatre training shines through every word he speaks. His timing is beautiful, not a word wasted, not a thought thrown away.'

There were others who saw the show, including Joe Murphy of the *Irish Echo*. No one knocked me and all agreed that my run at the Brooklyn Academy was too short. Nearing the end of the week Michael and I waited anxiously to hear from the Abbey management about our next engagement. We were part of the tour and, before we left Dublin, had received a preliminary list of venues at which we were to appear after New York. Our success at the Brooklyn Academy whetted our appetites for what lay ahead in places like Boston, Philadelphia and Washington.

We checked out of the Algonquin and booked into a cheaper place down the block. It turned out to be a hotel where the homeless on social welfare were housed. On my first day there, who should I see sitting in the lobby but an old actor, James L. O'Neill, who played the part of the schoolmaster in *Philadelphia, Here I Come!* on Broadway. He didn't know me and I realised from the deadness of his eye that he was in his dotage. I told him my name and he mistook me for Emmet Kelly, the great American circus clown. I tried again, mentioning the play we were in together and the Helen Hayes Theatre where we played.

'Sure, I know you,' he said with conviction, 'you were in the cast of *Abbie's Irish Rose*.' I left him to his dreams with his unquestioning eye staring into space.

Michael and I waited for the call. Someone from the Abbey had promised to come and talk to us and we hung around the lobby in case we missed him. While we were having a break in the coffee shop he did come but left again without seeing us. We did the most ridiculous things to pass the time, like trying to figure out how the Algonquin got its name. We called on the ghost of Myles Na Gopaleen to solve that one, and he did.

It seems that the Algonquin was first owned by Quinn, a Clareman, when Manhattan was sparsely populated. One day the Apache and Sioux Indians joined forces and invaded Manhattan. The people, fearing for their lives, flew through the Hudson tunnel into Queens. After some days the Clareman and his staff stole back to the island. They saw no Indians, and what was more important, no arrows. They took shelter where Times Square is now, and the Clareman sent one of his staff to reconnoitre around the hotel. The servant came back in high glee, and said, 'No Indians! I looked inside. All gone, Quinn.'

Dark clouds loomed large on our horizon. The Abbey must have failed to firm up our part of the tour, because we heard no word from the powers-that-be. Our inclusion in the visit had enabled the Abbey to fulfil the American Equity stipulation and get into the States. Now that they were here we felt that we weren't needed any more. This was a severe blow to us, abandoned as we were in New York with one hand as long as the next. Michael Colgan, ever a man of action, proposed that as we had a successful property on our hands, why not try and get some dates and do the show ourselves?

Then a gap came in the clouds and an angel appeared in the form of Paddy Noonan. Paddy owned the Rego Irish Records and Tapes Company and had issued some albums of mine. He was also the leader of a band which toured the States wherever Irish were to be found. We located Paddy in Garden City and he was willing to set up a number of dates for us in Irish neighbourhoods around New York State.

But what were we going to do for stage scenery? Michael hit on the idea of going to Harvey Lichtenstein at the Brooklyn Academy and asking him for our stage setting. It wasn't being brought back to Ireland and would wind up like all Broadway used scenery in a dump in New Jersey.

Lichtenstein turned up trumps. Unfortunately, Paddy Noonan's van wasn't large enough to take the set, except for the freestanding door and window, but we packed in all the furniture and props down to the last egg cup for the dresser. The time was short for publicity. Paddy arranged some outlets. Michael and I spoke on neighbourhood radio – a different station each night. We sat there relaxed in front of the microphone handing out news about Ireland and lauding our show to the moon.

As well as being engaged in publicity, Michael Colgan was the producer, the director, the stage manager and crew of the new venture. He also looked after the front of house and when necessary did his stint on tabs. Paddy Noonan brought in his musicians and we had what we called an 'afterture' of Irish music when the curtain came down.

Our first stand was on Friday 10 December at the Irish Centre in Mineola, New York State. The cottage furniture surrounded by black drapes, with the freestanding door and window and a mock-up fireplace, looked great when the curtain came across. The lighting wasn't the best and, bearing in mind what Bob Hope once said, if the artist is not lit properly his gags go for a burton, I feared the worst. But I used what light there was to my advantage and the show exceeded all expectations.

Saturday saw us in Holy Trinity Church at 20 Cumming's Street in the Bronx. The pastor introduced me, and Michael came to the dressing-room to say that I had better go out quick or the priest would have gone through the entire show. He had already told a story he had memorised from one of my albums, and another he had heard me tell on the radio that morning.

On Sunday we were at Catalpa, Ridgewood in Queens. My two aunts and near relations came back to see me and introduced me to one-time neighbours of my parents, some of whom had been in America since before the First World War. Our last two shows were held under the auspices of the Boston chapter of the Irish American Cultural Institute. We played in a high school theatre at Lexington, Waltham, Mass. Paddy Noonan stored the stage furniture and props in his garage and I used them in a subsequent visit to the States when Brian Collins, Abbey designer, accompanied me.

Back in Dublin I don't ever remember receiving an explanation from the Abbey management about the New York cock-up, but I do recall that there was a request that Michael and I hand over the meagre takings of the shows we did there. Naturally we demurred.

21

SUSPENDED!

During his term as artistic head at the Abbey, Alan Simpson directed a play by Constantine FitzGibbon called *The Devil at Work*. It was set in heaven and the theme was the creation of the world. Some of us actors played parts outside our range – I was the Archangel Gabriel. I don't think the hair hanging down in ringlets suited my cast of countenance. One ancient wag said I reminded him of a female newsreader he knew on 2RN (Ireland's first radio station, which broadcast from Denmark Street).

Maitias, from Paris, designed the celestial setting, and very beautiful it was too. One critic said, 'it was most elegant, most spectacular and a joy to look at'. At the opening the stage seemed resting on clouds with angels flying about. These heavenly beings were young people suitably costumed on swings. Into the angelic merry-go-round, falling from the skies of an upper heaven, dropped the Archangel Gabriel and the Archangel Michael, played by Geoff Golden. Before the curtain Geoff and I were hoisted high into the flies. Under our finery we wore parachute harnesses. A thin wire, invisible to the audience, was hooked into the back of the harness and we were winched aloft.

It was absolutely essential that we sat correctly into the tackling or agonies lay ahead. It was also very important that there was no twist in the wire, or the actor would spin around and back again. Our heads spun too in the dark upper world of ropes, catwalks and fly bars. The distance to the ground instilled terror, but what was most chilling was a plywood cut-out ground-row directly below; in an accident we were certain to be decapitated.

We were sent aloft ages before the curtain and we seemed to be hours dangling up there. At the dress rehearsal the director came to the front seats and, looking up, proclaimed that our angelic feet were showing. Heavenly hour! We had to be winched higher, which made the adrenalin race like mercury in our glands. Prior to this Geoff had been suspended without pay from the company for some misdemeanour, and on opening night he turned his head and said to me, 'Suspended for a month, and on my first night back I am suspended again!'

The gong sounded, and on the third reverberating stroke the curtain rose and Geoff and I floated down (I forget now if we spread our wings) into a cherubim- and seraphim-filled paradise and alighted on a rostrum upstage. Hands came from behind a masking drape and unhooked us from the wire. God, were we happy to find our feet on firm ground as we walked down and mingled with the other angels. With music, lighting, costumes and a heavenly setting, it was a wonderful sight. A member of the audience told me afterwards that Geoff's descent and mine looked like two figures from the famous painting of the Assumption going the wrong way.

On a bugle call from Gabriel the heavenly host got busy. Architect and engineer angels began work at the drawing board mapping out our wonderful world. The seas were soon filled with fish and the earth populated with animals. The Garden of Eden was created, and the last thing we see at the close of the play is Eve throwing that unfortunate, for us, apple to Adam.

In between there was much activity, and as each animal was planned, a painted cut-out of the creature was run on a wire upstage with a witty comment from the angels on each invention. On beholding a strange shape whizzing across one angel inquired, 'What's this?' and was told, 'That's a yak — useful for crosswords.'

There was also the angels' revolt. Desmond Cave played Lucifer, and Harry Brogan, as Zerubabbe, was one of the dirtiest looking devils you could wish to see. *The Irish Times* described Alan Simpson's production as excellent and the Abbey Company as grand. David Nowlan continued: 'Eric Sweeney's music and Leslie Scott's lighting add to the air of sophistication with which the whole production is endowed, and it is for this sophistication — not all that commonly seen in theatrical terms in the Abbey — that the evening is ultimately to be commended. Had we been told, even a year ago, that we would have seen its like in the Abbey, we might not have believed it. To be believed it must be seen.'

22

STONE MAD

Apart from Tomás Mac Anna and Frank Dermody I worked with many directors at the Abbey. Ray McAnally, who had left the permanent company for a while, came back to direct. I was fortunate to be in his production of *Kolbe*, set in a concentration camp and written by Desmond Forristal. Clive Geraghty played the part of Kolbe, a Polish priest who sacrifices his life so that another inmate of the camp may live. I was a Jewish tailor. Shaven-headed and emaciated looking, Kolbe and I languished in an Auschwitz prison cell. As the Jew and the Catholic priest prepare for death the Jew, with the characteristic humour of his race, suggests that they hear each other's confession.

I ever relished working with Ray McAnally. He got performances out of me which I didn't think I was capable of. He directed *The Loves of Cass Maguire* by Brian Friel and gave me the role of Mr Ingram. I was fortunate to be around at that time and to have the privilege of appearing in so many of Friel's plays. To the other practitioners who excel in the art of play-writing in Ireland give dukedoms, earldoms and knight them, but for Friel reserve the jewelled crown. He is the king.

Like Ray McAnally, Joe Dowling was an Abbey actor who became a director. I remember the two Friel plays in which he cast me. One was *Translations* at the Abbey and the other *Fathers and Sons* at the Gate. It was a joy to work with him. His ability to reassure an actor abated the terror which always seizes me at my first entrance from the wings. Acting is a nerve-racking business. Fellow players have likened opening nights to going over the top in the Great War.

It was Lelia Doolan who introduced me to Patrick Mason. 'This young Englishman,' she said, 'comes to the Abbey as our new voice teacher.' I couldn't help remarking, with as much humour as I could muster, 'When the conquered speak in the tones of the conqueror the conquest is complete.' Patrick laughed heartily, assuring me that no attempt would be made to change the tenor of the native lilt.

Patrick, who at first assisted Hugh Hunt in his production of *The Well of the Saints,* went on to become a director of international repute. He directed Noel Pearson's and the Abbey production of Brian Friel's *Dancing at Lughnasa* in Dublin, London and New York, where the play won Tony Awards for the author, director and players. Patrick is now artistic director at the Abbey.

I remember I was in his production of *The Cherry Orchard* in which I played the part of the old retainer, Firs. The play was in a new translation by Michael Frayn. When he came to a rehearsal one day Patrick asked me to repeat for him what I said about speaking in the tones of the conqueror. I was a bit embarrassed but I did it. Like Patrick, Michael Frayn took no umbrage. The British are bricks when it comes to tolerance, and he agreed with me that small communities should try and hold on to their distinctiveness at all costs.

My last appearance with the Abbey was in a play directed by Patrick Mason. It was *The Only True History of Lizzie Finn* by Sebastian Barry. I had known Sebastian Barry ever since I had been in his *Boss Grady's Boys* at the Peacock Theatre in 1988. That play turned out to be the talk of the town and a great favourite with the critics. 'Barry's writing has a subtlety which puts *Boss Grady's Boys* into a different league from the vast majority of plays that have been written about rural Ireland since Synge,' Tim Harding said in the *Sunday Press*.

Of Jim Norton and me, who played the principal parts, David Nowlan said in *The Irish Times*: ' . . . two of the best performances seen on the Dublin stage this year . . . seldom have two characterisations been so nicely balanced in emotion and intelligence. Seldom have words been so well spoken to convey feeling and clarity of thought, silences and actions full of mutual communications.'

Caroline Fitzgerald's superbly sensitive and imaginative production was talked about in the *Sunday Tribune*, and in the *Sunday Independent* Hugh Leonard said the play craved to be seen. Later I was in Sebastian's *Prayers of Sherkin* and saw his magical *The Steward of Christendom* at the Gate with Donal McCann.

Sean McCarthy directed me in Seamus Murphy's *Stone Mad*, a one-man show which had been adapted for the stage by Fergus Linehan and was set in a monumental mason's yard. In the book Seamus tells of his apprenticeship as a stonecutter and describes his work with a gallant gallery of eccentric craftsmen, men with names like the Gargoyle, the Tumbler, the Goban, the Dust, Bulltoes and Danny Melt.

Bronwen Casson designed a very realistic stoneyard (it won her an award) with examples of work in progress – statues, Celtic crosses and headstones – together with all the appurtenances of the trade, including bankers to work on and a small forge. The setting was in the round in the Peacock Theatre and the audience had ringside seats as I worked the stone and told the tales which have made Seamus Murphy's *Stone Mad* the classic that it is.

To give a sense of authenticity to my work with mallet and chisel I went and studied with the stonecutters in Roe O'Neill's quarries in Ballyedmonduff near the foot of the Dublin Mountains. Having worked as a carpenter in my youth gave me a decided facility in the handling and use of tools. In no time, under expert tutelage, I was able to block off the waste on a Celtic cross, and I mastered to a degree the cutting of letters on a monument.

Beforehand each evening I arranged the pieces of stone I had to work on during my almost two hours on stage. One job was the cutting of an inscription on a headstone: 'Walter Poplin. Died March twenty-fifth, nineteen sixty-three. Aged sixty years. RIP.' (Walter Poplin was Big Maggie's husband in the play of that name by John B. Keane, and that's what was written on the note she handed to the stonecutter Byrne the day of his funeral.) Another task was the sculpting of a design on a Celtic cross.

I left the using of the forge for the opening of part two. Then I heated a chisel in a gas flame in the wings. I came on stage in the blackout with the glowing red chisel concealed from view, and beat it to a cutting edge on the anvil as the lights came up. When finished I plunged the hot iron into water, making a sizzling sound and sending up a cloud of steam. Whatever about the interpretation of the lines, the portraying of a craftsman doing his work with precision and fluidity gave me immense satisfaction. And to my mind nothing like it had been done on the stage before.

Among the messages of goodwill on opening night there was a note from Joe Dowling the artistic director. It read: 'Warmest congratulations on *Stone Mad*, and every good wish for tonight and the run. You had great courage to undertake

such a mammoth job, and you have scored a major achievement. It is a personal triumph for you and the theatre is
deeply grateful to you. Good luck.'

Seamus Murphy's widow, Mairéad, and her son Colm were
in the theatre, which made me a little apprehensive. The only
one who noticed this was Con Houlihan. Writing in the
Evening Press he said I was nervous at the outset but before
long I had the audience eating out of my hand. The critics
didn't know how to describe the evening. It wasn't a play. I
suppose you could call it a 'docudrama', a visit by the
audience to a stoneyard where I populated the scene with
Seamus Murphy's celebrated 'stonies', told their tales, did
their work on stone and paused to blow the chisel dust from
the lettering on the limestone tablet.

After a successful run at the Peacock we went on tour.
Strong hands shifted the Celtic cross, the holy water font,
the slabs of stone and the angel with the broken wing. I was
bockety at the knees with fright going on stage the opening
night at the Everyman Theatre in Cork city, where Seamus
lived and worked, and where he had a legion of friends and
admirers.

I needn't have worried. The big-hearted Leesiders took a
shine to me, and Maureen Fox writing in the *Cork Examiner*
said: '*Stone Mad* is sheer joy.' She liked my playing of the
part: ' . . . those who were lucky enough to have known
Seamus Murphy time and time again during the evening must
have felt as if he himself was speaking.' She also liked Sean
McCarthy's sensitive direction and Bronwen Casson's stage
design, which set the seal on a wonderful evening.

23

FIELD DAY AND THE KING'S HEAD

I got a chance again to use the sculpting skills I had picked up in Roe O'Neill's quarry when I was cast with Maura in Tom Murphy's *Brigit*, a play for television. Tom, whose praises are sung though I be silent, is one of our foremost writers in the theatre. I was in his *A Crucial Week in the Life of a Grocer's Assistant*, directed by Alan Simpson.

Tom's play *Brigit* is a delicate and very moving piece of writing in which a proud though amateur craftsman, the part I played, accepts a commission a little outside his range. It is to carve a statue of Saint Brigit for the nuns to replace the one which was knocked over by a clumsy postulant and broken into smithereens. The Reverend Mother tries the religious repositories but can't find a plaster representation of the native saint.

The craftsman takes on the job and carves the figure in bog oak. He works at it day and night. He pours his soul into the creation. He sometimes sings as the big mallet drives the chisel into the wood and when darkness falls his wife and his grandchildren in turn hold the paraffin lamp to throw light on his work. When it is finished the nuns are dubious about the somewhat crude but honest piece of sculpture. However, after consultation with the parish priest, they accept the statue on condition that it be given a coat of paint.

The craftsman, incensed at the idea of painting the beautiful dark bog oak, older, he says, than St Brigit herself, takes the figure from its niche and brings it home. He sits by the hearth gazing into the flames, his hand moving over the work he has so lovingly carved. In a fit of rage he is about to throw it in the fire. His wife prevents him and puts the statue in a place of honour in the kitchen. Her name is Brigit too and, tearfully, she says she sees some of herself in her husband's work.

The play was imaginatively directed by Noel Ó Briain, and I believe it was the last drama to be screened by RTÉ. That was 1988. The following year it won an award at the Celtic Nations Television Festival.

During the troubled times in Northern Ireland, I worked with Stephen Rea in the Field Day Company, when he directed Chekhov's *Three Sisters* in a translation by Brian Friel. I played the part of Ivan Chebutykin, and when the dizzy hour of my first scene came on opening night in the Guildhall in Derry, a British Army helicopter sat in the sky above the stage and all but drowned me out. I had to strive with might and main to make myself heard. When the infernal machine chugged off at the end of the scene I got a hand, more, I think, in appreciation of my fight against the army of occupation than for any gold-medal acting on my part.

One day during rehearsals in the Guildhall there was a bomb alert. All out and down three flights of stairs into the open ground. The adjoining houses and shops emptied into the street and people made for the open space around the hall. I saw John Hume in the crowd. In time word came as to the position of the car bomb. All eyes were directed towards an archway maybe a hundred yards away. Suddenly there was an almighty explosion which left a sickening feeling at the butt of the stomach.

Black smoke billowed from the archway and at its centre there was a red glow tinged with blue and purple. Faces drained of colour and there was a moment of absolute stillness. Some people had to be supported because of the shock. There was a public house at the side of the Guildhall, its windows covered with corrugated iron sheets to save them from flying bomb splinters. We went in there. As the effects of the blast wore off, some had drinks and some had coffee.

There were two English ladies who worked in the show, a mother and daughter. One was in design and the other a costumier. As a delayed reaction to the explosion the daughter fainted, but the mother was unshaken. She had been through the bombing in London during the Second World War.

The proprietor was most kind to us and some of the actors used to drop in there when the show was over and stay after hours. One night late, two RUC constables came into the bar. They didn't take any names but stood at the back in the shadows. When he saw them, Colm Meaney, who played Captain Vassily Solyony in the show, engaged me in a very loud conversation in Irish of dubious ancestry. He was a little in his cups and meant to be provocative. It made for an uneasy atmosphere. After a while the two RUC men left, and at the door one of them turned on his heel and, addressing Meaney, said, '*Oiche mhaith!*'

While we were in Derry, BBC Television did a documentary on the work of Field Day. When the camera crew came to my lodgings to interview me I was setting out for the launderette. That would be fine, the director said. They would talk to me in the car. The interview was done as we drove along and while I was putting the clothes in the washing machine. Mine was the last piece of filming and immediately afterwards the crew were to drive to Belfast and back to Britain.

They left, and with my laundry washed and dried I was walking down the street in the Waterside. Putting my hand on the lapel of my jacket I found the miniature microphone which they had forgotten to take. The battery was still in my back pocket, the connecting flex hanging visibly from my trousers belt.

A twinge of panic as I thought of the explaining I would have to do if stopped by the police. The lilt of my southern brogue wouldn't help. I spoke into the microphone, calling the crew and telling them what had happened. I wasn't sure if they could hear me or if they had already left. Noticing a public house nearby I gave them the name of the street and the pub and said I could be found there. Just then a police Land Rover came into view and I held my breath until it had passed me.

I went into the pub, turned up my coat collar to hide the microphone and tucked the flex under my belt. When I ordered a pint – it must have been my accent – the publican eyed me suspiciously. There was nobody in the room off the bar. I went in there, sipped the pint and every now and then talked in a low voice into the broadcasting unit. After what seemed an eternity the BBC people crowded into where I was sitting, and before the publican could see what was happening they had relieved me of their precious sound equipment. A short without a chaser and they were off. Because of their English accents and their delight at our meeting, the publican showed a new interest in me. We became very friendly and talked about the troubles.

I nodded agreement when he condemned the outrages of the republicans, but watching his expression out of the corner of my eye, I knew he was somewhat perplexed by my accent.

During my stay with the Abbey the management was very generous in giving me time off. As well as playing with Field Day and the Irish Theatre Company, I went on trips to America with my storytelling shows and appeared on Irish and British television. The summer of 1977 saw me in the King's Head in London. The King's Head is a dinner-type theatre and is carried on in a large room at the rear of the pub of that name. It is run by Dan Crawford, a Canadian who directs many of the plays himself.

I played there in *Da* by Hugh Leonard. I was in the name part in one of the best roles written for an actor this century. The play was directed by Robert Gillespie, a demanding taskmaster. His hard work paid off and the play was a dazzling success. We cornered all the critics. Speaking of the character of Da the *Daily Telegraph* wrote: ' . . . Leonard has the theatrical cunning to make brilliant fun of this crazy individualist, who is uncannily impersonalised by Éamon Kelly.'

As the King's Head is on the fringe of London's theatre world, the actors are not well paid. They work for the lower salary in the hope that the play may transfer. To help me on this reduced salary Dan Crawford offered to provide lodgings for me. I got a shakedown upstairs in the pub, but the room was too near the kitchen and I couldn't stand the cooking smells.

Seeing my discomfort, one of the pub staff gave me his flat a few streets away. It was a one-roomed basement accommodation with no window, just a glass door leading to an open area. I was afraid to open the door at night to let in air in case someone barged in on me from the street.

On my arrival there the caretaker viewed me with suspicion, thinking, I suppose, that the occupant of the flat was subletting. On my second night, at about two o'clock, there was a loud pounding on the door. I opened it and a man and his wife dashed into the room. The gentleman, who turned out to be the Polish landlord, was in a tearing temper. His wife, a big blonde, her face pushed back as if she had it pressed against a window pane, carried a large handbag from which I expected to get a belt any minute.

Accoutred as I was in crumpled pyjamas, I calmed them down as best I could. I explained that I was in a play in the King's Head and that one of the staff, the tenant of this flat, had let me stay for a while. They didn't believe my story: I was an intruder. I had a poster of the play pinned to the back of the door and I showed them my name, the first under the title and high enough to be well out of reach of a dog's pee no matter how low it was placed. The name on my passport, which I always take to London, agreed with the poster.

I gave them a synopsis of my theatrical career, with snippets of my work on Broadway and on tour in the States — I am sure they thought they were making my acquaintance on the way down. They were mollified slightly and withdrew, warning me that subletting was out of the question and to quit when I got other accommodation.

I told Dan Crawford of my experience and he gave me a flat belonging to a woman friend of his who would be out of London for some time. All I had to do in return was to water the nineteen plants and to care for and feed the cat. For days I didn't see the cat, but then on putting my hand in the hot press I felt her soft fur. She mewed defensively and then spat at me, but after I had fed her a few times we became firm friends. It was a first-floor flat and in time she got to know the hour at which I would be coming home from the theatre and sat out on the windowsill to mew me a welcome.

The flat was spacious, two rooms, two beds. It was pleasingly decorated with a large colour drawing of Queen Meadhbh by Jim Fitzpatrick as a centrepiece. I invited Maura and Sinéad over from Dublin. They stayed for a few weeks, and Eoin and Brian, then about eighteen and seventeen, came to London. They explored the city on the Underground, went on a pilgrimage to Wembley Stadium and sat on the Queen's seat.

After the run of *Da* at the King's Head I put on my one-man storytelling show, *In My Father's Time*, at the same theatre. Michael Colgan came over from Dublin to prepare it for the stage, and with the *Irish Post* and the *Cork Weekly Examiner* behind me, a good sprinkling of Irish people swelled the audiences each night. I couldn't have wished for a more intimate space, with a perfect acoustic, in which to do the show.

Mention of familiar placenames or references to scenes of yore and summers long ago would cause a throat-clearing 'ahem' from Irish pockets in the audience. One night a description of an emigration parting at a railway station back home gave rise to a muffled 'Divine Jesus' from the front seat. A quick change to comedy softened the catch in the heart, and laughter again ran through the auditorium.

A one-man entertainment can be a lonely commitment for the actor. He misses the company of the other players, with no one to talk to before the show or during the interval. But the fall of the curtain brought people to the dressing-room, and I met many a son and daughter of neighbours I grew up with in Kerry.

One night I had company on stage when Dan Crawford's black tomcat walked on and sat on his bottom a few feet away from me. He took no interest in the folklore I was dispensing but licked his right front paw and proceeded to wash his face. Delighted giggles kept at a low pitch did not disturb him but I knew that his presence was the end of me. I had lost the interest of the audience, but I gradually regained it by addressing the story to the cat in as soothing and seductive a manner as I was capable of. It worked. A two-hander with a cat, and the audience silently loved it. Sometimes, at some telling remark, he stopped the circular washing motion of his face and, with the paw resting over one ear, turned and looked at me.

The end of the story brought a burst of applause which startled the cat. He looked at the audience, spat once and disappeared into the wings. It was a strange and eerie experience where an animal in all its naturalness took the spotlight off the action and stole the show. While I was on stage thereafter the cat was confined to Dan's living quarters.

Many years later I was back in the King's Head in a production of *Philadelphia, Here I Come!* directed by Dan Crawford. I was in the part of the father, which I had played in Dublin, Broadway and Shaftesbury Avenue twenty-eight years before. This time we moved from the King's Head and it was nice to be told by producer Bill Kenwright that my performance was the deciding factor in bringing the play into the West End.

We were in Wyndham's Theatre, hard by Leicester Square, while another play of Friel's, *Dancing at Lughnasa*, was running in a house down the street. We were doing fine until the IRA caught up with us in the autumn of 1992. Then the bombings began in the centre of London. These tragic events did not affect the theatre attendances at first, but as time went on and the count of the bombings came to fourteen, there were some empty seats in the stalls.

Just a hundred yards from Wyndham's Theatre where we

were playing, a bomb shattered the Sussex Arms public house. Five people were injured in the blast and one, David Heifer, lay critically ill in hospital. The following day David died. He came from Luton and was thirty years of age.

What had David to do with the Ireland of the North or South? What had he to do with the invasions or the plantation of Ulster? In what way was he guilty of any crime against the Irish people that he should give his life? He was one of the many in England, including children, who were killed by bombs planted by the young men and women of the IRA. We read in the paper that David carried a donor card and in death he gave to more than one person the gift of life.

The only gesture we could make was to place a bouquet of flowers with the hundreds of other tributes on the fallen rubble of the Sussex Arms, with the message, 'In memory of David. From the cast of *Philadelphia, Here I Come!*'

24

WHERE HUBERT HUMPHREY
AND PRESIDENT FORD SLEPT

In the early summer of 1981 I went to America on a story-telling tour organised by Paddy Noonan of New York. I took Brian Collins, the Abbey Theatre designer, with me to set the stage and act as lighting man and tour manager. In New York, while we were preparing to go out on the road, we stayed in an old-fashioned hotel not far from the United Nations building. Because I was commissioned to do a new story-telling show for the Peacock when I came back to Dublin, I got up every morning at six and wrote and rehearsed for two and a half hours. I wouldn't have done it at home, but I have always found the air in America more bracing, urging one on to activity.

We used the stage furniture and props which Paddy Noonan had stored in his garage after the Abbey bicentennial tour in 1975. These included a freestanding door and window, and to give ourselves a homely cottage set Brian and I built a fireplace. This could be folded flat to fit in Paddy's van, and with a full cargo, Brian, I and a driver set out on a tour of places in New England. We visited Boston,

Springfield and Worcester.

There was an Irish contact person in each place, and in Worcester it was Jack Finnegan. We slept in his mother's house one night. She was away in California. Next day we were taken to Jack's conference centre, a secluded place deep in the woods. The entrance had no gate, but tied to a post in the middle of a broad opening was a ferocious-looking alsatian on a long chain which enabled him to cover the distance to the piers at each side. Hard by was a helicopter pad in the trees.

Jack rented the centre to political parties and big business combines. A feature of it was a miniature Roman arena-type room with stepped seats looking down on a blazing fire, where men sat draped in large towels after a stint in the jacuzzi. Here Brian and I sat, similarly accoutred, with Irish American men. It was the time of the Northern Ireland hunger strike and the talk was about Bobby Sands. His ordeal affected them greatly. 'If he dies,' one man said, striking his fist in his open palm, 'oh, if he dies!'

We saw the conference and various meeting rooms. We visited the bar and had a meal in the restaurant. That night Brian slept where Hubert Humphrey had laid down to rest, and across the corridor I slept in President Ford's bed. There was a step down to the john in that room and Jack Finnegan told me that the President, who tended to trip himself up, fell into the place to a chorus from his bodyguard – 'He has done it again!'

In the closet Jack showed me the red telephone which, when plugged in at Ford's bedside, was the hotline to Moscow and to the man with his finger on the nuclear button. Finnegan had arranged a radio interview for me at the unearthly hour of 2 a.m., when there would be a hook-up coast to coast. At that time the telephone woke me and, snugly ensconced in the President's bed, I spoke to the nation.

When we went to the midwest and the west coast we had to forget about the set and stage furniture. We got a trunk not too large to be taken on a plane and packed into it essential props like the oil lamp, delph for the dresser and objects for the mantelpiece, or whatever versions of them we would get at each centre.

On arriving at a community theatre or hall, Brian went to the scene dock and prop room and it was surprising what he came up with by way of stage setting. Two old bookcases of different sizes, one on top of the other, made a dresser. He'd maybe fish out a door and a window. With a few boards and sturdy scantlings he made a fireplace with a mantelshelf and gave the lot a coat of fast-drying paint.

There were nearly always black drapes to half-circle the result of his endeavours, and his intelligence and imagination gave me a credible, well lit scene in which to work at every centre.

In Lansing, Michigan, we were at the little theatre in the university and Brian got very believable furniture for the stage from the folk museum nearby. Here we were both called upon to talk to the drama class. Brian spoke about design and I about my work in the theatre.

From Lansing to Grand Rapids. It was a domestic flight in a plane with a seating capacity of little more than that of the Killarney to Rathmore bus. When the craft came down it seemed about to shake to pieces as it ground to a halt on the runway. In Grand Rapids we stayed with John Tully, a lawyer and possibly the tallest man in America. There was a great gathering of Irish people in his house after the show, some of whom hadn't seen Ireland since they had left maybe twenty years before, and others who had never seen it. When we told them how things stood at home, the conversation turned to the Northern troubles. This was always so when we met Irish Americans. The younger men were very passionate about the North, and crew like fighting cocks.

In Austin, Texas, I was to play in the university theatre, which was in the round. This meant some changes in the presentation. In the house where we stayed, when the owner Kevin O'Connell and his wife went away for the day, we took a table and chairs out to the lawn and re-ran the show with an in-the-round audience in mind.

During this operation we forgot to close the door or to put the mosquito screen in place, with the result that when the lady of the house came back she found the place full of flies. 'Who let the bugs in?' she demanded. We were abject in our apologies while the insect repellent went into action.

Brian, with assistance from the crew, readied and lit the stage and the show worked like a dream. Anyway I had plenty of practice at playing in the round at the Peacock Theatre at home.

Dr Padraig Houlahan, who was with the American Space Programme, met us here, and he and Kevin O'Connell brought us to Maggie Mac's for a drink. Maggie's was a long narrow establishment with a sprinkling of Irish. A small country and western band played at the end. The lady vocalist came to the microphone and said, 'Bobby Sands is very low tonight. He is in a coma now!' There was a silence and she added, 'I'll sing an Irish song.' What she sang was, 'I have heard the mavis singing'.

Next day, Kevin O'Connell drove us to San Antonio, where I met Maureen Halligan. She took me to see Ronnie Ibbs. The theatre where they work, and where I played, is part of a convent university, a fairly big auditorium but we very nearly filled it. Afterwards we had a meal across the street with the nuns and Father O'Gorman.

New Orleans by air was our next stop. It is a beautiful city and my favourite American place after New York. Strangely enough, the name of the university dean who welcomed us was Éamon Kelly. The evening paper said, 'Stand Up the Real Éamon Kelly'. My name went on parchment as the Mayor, Ernest N. Maoil, conferred on me the title of International Honorary Citizen of New Orleans.

We were back in New York in time to board the boat for Bermuda. This was a cruise on the SS *Doric*, with a full complement of Irish Americans, arranged by Manhattan travel agents. Paddy Noonan with his orchestra and yours truly were on board to entertain them. The *Doric* was an Italian liner with an Italian crew. The chaplin was Italian also and on the first morning at Mass he wished us all to 'half nice scruise'.

Working at sea was a new experience. I had played in many places, from large theatres on Broadway and in London to village halls in Ireland and Newfoundland. I did a show in the open air in County Cork with arc-lamps hanging from trees around a dancing deck. Cars on the rising ground circled the space with their headlights on the small stage. There was a rookery nearby and I competed with the disturbed occupants. An old lady sitting beside my wife, and unaware of Maura's identity, said as she pointed at me, 'Is that him now? Sainted hour, sure, my old man is as good looking as him!'

On board the *Doric*, the chapel in the morning was the theatre at night. Paddy Noonan and his musicians played there. I did two shows on the way out, two on the way back, and one when we were docked at Hamilton in Bermuda. I had lots of time off during the day to sit in the bar, read by the swimming pool or sunbathe on the upper deck. There were plenty of people to talk to, men who had left Ireland

and who wished to talk about it. Sometimes late at night when Paddy Noonan played in the ship's lounge I did a ten-to fifteen-minute stint at the microphone.

I noticed that some of the passengers were grossly overweight and at mealtimes these were the people who ate as if there were no tomorrows. Their eyes widened and they 'ooh'ed and 'aah'ed at the food before them. We had breakfast, lunch and dinner, and coffees in between, and late at night long tables on the mid-deck groaned under the weight of mouthwatering delicacies. Over the loudspeakers passengers were invited to bring their cameras. They did, and photographed the entire pâtisserie before anyone had time to sink a tooth in it.

We spent some days on the island of Bermuda with its beautiful beaches. I had forgotten my bathing suit and bought one in Hamilton, as well as a sports jacket, all for seventy-one dollars. The sea water had the quality of white wine. One day, lying on the golden sand after a dip, we heard on Brian's radio that the Pope had been shot at in Rome.

A striking feature of the place was the white roofs of the houses. They seemed to be made of concrete. Each house had a huge tank to catch the rainfall as running water was scarce on the island. We fished out and found the house where Tom Moore lived when he was governor there.

We set sail again, north to New York. We docked at the West Pier, where thousands of Irish had first set foot in America. We bade a fond farewell to the many friends we had made on board, and, after a night's rest, Brian and I had three more centres to do in the State of New York: Indwood, Scarsdale in Suffolk County, and one in a city hotel. When the owner of that hostelry saw my stage effects being trundled through the lobby, and when he beheld the dilapidated table, dresser and *súgán* chairs, he threw a fit and roared, 'Take them away! I didn't order such garbage!'

That show over, we were in the air again, going west to San Francisco, a city in its own way every bit as distinctive as New Orleans. We saw the famous tramcars, which are powered from a central electric rail in the street. Don't ask me why people don't get electrocuted by stepping on the rail, but it seems an insulated plunger reaches through a continuous slot to the power which is cunningly concealed below. The trams are very popular and when they are full, passengers crowd the entry platforms and hang from grips over running boards at the side. We rode on one down to the bay, took a boat around Alcatraz, the famous prison island, and under the arches of the Golden Gate Bridge.

The Irish have a fine centre in San Francisco. It is to this meeting place that our country's emigrants flock in the early morning of the first and third Sundays of September to hear the RTÉ broadcast of the hurling and football All-Ireland finals.

It is a well equipped place with a large hall. So large, indeed, that Brian, not trusting the acoustics, asked me to use a microphone. This instrument ties me to one position. I prefer to move in the set, using the chair by the fire, at the table and the dresser. I introduce as much unobtrusive business as I can, and I have been known, in Dublin anyway, to fall to repairing a horse's collar and winkers.

In San Francisco Brian enabled me to move about freely by getting me a radio device with a battery in my hip pocket and a tiny microphone on my lapel.

We played in Sacramento too, where it became so hot on stage that I nearly lost my breath. Here I met an ex-pupil from my teaching days in Listowel Technical School. He told me he was running a small ranch.

The tour over, we returned to New York where I got

presents for Maura and Sinéad. At the airport Paddy Noonan paid us. The proceeds when divided up didn't seem all that great; we admitted we'd have earned as much working in the theatre in Dublin. Travel and other expenses were high but we wouldn't have missed the trip, and, as Brian said, not everyone in Ireland could claim to have slept where Hubert Humphrey and President Ford had laid their weary heads.

25

A STEPPE IN THE LEFT DIRECTION

Like the *Skibbereen Eagle*, the Abbey had had its eye on Russia for many a long day. Its actors had played in Edinburgh, London, New York and elsewhere, and it would be another feather in their caps to appear in the famed Arts Theatre of Moscow.

In Vincent Dowling's term as artistic director an invitation came to play in Leningrad (as it was then) and Moscow. The plays the Russians asked for were *The Great Hunger*, a drama by Tom MacIntyre based on Patrick Kavanagh's poem of that name, and *The Field* by John B. Keane.

John B. is the people's playwright. For many years, from Valentia to Belturbet, the rafters of parochial halls have rung to the raciness of his poetic outpourings. From the early 1980s he enjoyed an amazing popularity at the Abbey Theatre. I was in *Sharon's Grave*, which was presented there by the Irish Theatre Company when Christopher Fitz Simon was its artistic director. The play was directed by Sheila Richards, who found some of the Kerry dialogue a little strange. I had to plead with her to keep in expressions like 'above in the room' and 'below in the kitchen', because, as she said, the set in which we played had no upstairs.

In 1984 I appeared as Morrisheen Brick in *The Man from Clare*. John B. brings the footballers of Cuas in County Clare across the Shannon to play the Bealabawn team in Kerry. The play was directed by Patrick Laffan and had Ray McAnally in the cast.

Then in 1985 came *Sive*. It was first produced by Listowel Drama Group in 1959 and had a long journey to the Abbey through the halls and ballrooms of rural Ireland. It was directed at the National Theatre by Ben Barnes, with Marie Kean, Catherine Byrne, John Olohan, Meave Germaine and Donal Farmer among those in the cast.

Sive has a chorus of two travelling men, Pats Bocock and his son Carthalawn. I was Pats and Macdara Ó Fáharta played my son. While on stage, they both comment on the night's proceedings in song and in story. Carthalawn plays the *bodhrán* and Pats beats time on the floor with his blackthorn stick. In Act Two, which is the eve of a wedding, there is porter in the house and father and son lower two bottles without taking the containers off their heads.

On opening night, to my exhortation of 'Your best! Your almighty best!' Carthalawn hit the bodhrán with such vigour that he drove his knuckles through the skin, but with amazing alacrity and without missing a note he continued to beat out the rhythm on the rim of the drum. There were many revivals of *Sive* – a play with which to make music on a box-office till. My last appearance in it was with an Abbey cast at the Gaiety in 1994.

John B. came to see us once while the play was in rehearsal, but he and director Ben Barnes met and talked over the production beforehand. They became firm friends and 1987 saw Ben directing *The Field*, which had first been produced in Dublin by Phyllis Ryan's Gemini Productions in November 1965 with Ray McAnally as the Bull McCabe. There had also been an earlier presentation at the Abbey with Joe Lynch in the part of the Bull. In Ben Barnes's production the Bull was played by Niall Tóibín, and a vicious bloody Bull he was too. My heart raced with fear as he and his son Tadhg (Brendan Conroy) killed the man who would take their precious field from them.

Big Maggie, with Brenda Fricker in the title role, completed the Keane trilogy directed by Ben Barnes at the Abbey, but it was *The Field* that was to be seen again in a far off land.

Maura and I were to play Mr and Mrs Dandy McCabe. On Saturday 6 February 1988 we packed our bags for Russia. 'Air your woollies for Arbour Hill!' was the call to active young republicans approaching winter in Kerry in the 1940s, and we made sure that only warm clothing was in our luggage. I bought a heavy long black topcoat in the Blarney Woollen Mills in Nassau Street. I had a Russian hat, synthetic fur of course, and with a warm scarf and gloves I was ready to face the severest Russian winter.

On Sunday at 2.30 p.m. we boarded a coach for Limerick and Shannon from the front of the Abbey. The two pubs opposite, the Plough and the Flowing Tide, put up a free drink for thirsty travellers. Danny O'Sullivan, the barman in the Tide, regretted he wasn't going with us. He made me down a vodka to get me in training in case of a Moscow pub crawl.

We stayed overnight in the Two Mile Inn at Limerick and after breakfast we crowded into the coach for Shannon. Our tour manager distributed visas and customs forms, and there was much writing to be done as we drove along. 'Any firearms? Any antiques?' Myself maybe.

The check-in at the airport was a bit hectic. There were the casts of two plays, the crew, the lighting and design people, the touring manager John Costigan and the theatre manager Martin Fahy as well as representatives of the press. A premature announcement to board at Gate 4 sent us all scurrying towards departures, but it turned out that we had plenty of time. Time to go to duty free, pose for photographs and have interviews with press and radio.

'And how do you feel now, Éamon, going to play in the Moscow Arts Theatre?'

'I feel,' I said, 'like an old Kerry parish priest going to say Mass in the Vatican.'

A while in the air and drinks were passed around. I opted for a vodka — neat. It was heart and belly warming. Reds throw it back in one gulp. I sipped it and waited for our first taste of Russian food, only to find that the lunch packs were made up at Shannon. There were the old familiars, Kerry Gold butter, *Siúcra Éireann* and Galtee cheese.

I sat by the window at the Kildare side as we flew eastwards. It was a beautiful day. The cold land and seas of northern Europe unfolded before me. Gradually the light faded. The days were short and darkness was not far away. Then we were above the clouds and the slanting sun still shone on a floor of cotton wool. As we neared Leningrad we lost height and I could make out roads stretching along the snow covered countryside.

The dark portions I took to be forests. As we descended, the roads seemed to be deserted and we must have gone the breadth of Munster before I saw my first car, the headlights making the snow in front a little whiter. As we neared the city the traffic increased to two or three cars, never more, moving between the clusters of lights that indicated the villages.

We made a perfect descent, like gliding down on a feather tick, and a perfect landing. We were bused from the runway to an austere arrival hall. The passport check was very strict. The official, who seemed to be in army uniform, not only looked at me but peered closer through half-closed eyes and back to the photograph. He motioned me to turn round and take off my hat. Grudgingly, I thought, he let me pass on.

There was a long delay for our luggage to come through. One hour and twenty minutes. John Costigan had warned us about it, having been here before. We had to go through customs again even though our baggage had been checked at Shannon by Soviet personnel. Then there was a big rigmarole about currency and more writing to do.

At last we were in the coach and heading for the city centre. It was not as bright as O'Connell Street. We drew up at the Hotel Europe, a stocky building of three or four storeys with a frowning cornice. Inside, the large lobby with its pillars, plaster decor and gold painted figures reminded me of old-time hotels I had seen in New York.

The riddle of the rooms was sorted out. Sharing was the order of the day. Some resented this, but I was not complaining. My wife and I were in 236, a real relic of oul' decency: not a room, a suite, with a charming sitting-room, beautifully furnished and with a television set, a radio (not working) and a phone. A bedroom opened off, and a bathroom with glazed tiles and brass fittings that must have been put in place before I was born. The door key was huge and the lock so ancient that it took some time to get the knack of opening it.

Dinner was to be at 9.30. I had a drink first in the currency bar. There were also currency shops where goods could be obtained for sterling or dollars. I had a nip of brandy and needed it at two degrees below. It cost me £1.75. As I paid the barman I said I could have got it for less in the Flowing Tide. 'Spaseeba,' he said and filled a beer for a thirsty tourist.

Conor O'Clery of *The Irish Times* dropped in and was suitably chuffed by my remark that the Abbey's visit to Russia was a 'steppe in the left direction'.

The dinner brought me back to a Listowel eating house during race week in the 1940s. All manner of servants helped at table, from fully fledged waiters to women in high boots dressed for the snow. The food was fine and a bottle of Georgian red wine cost four roubles – you'd have change out of a fiver. And so to bed. I bid the porter good-night in Russian. He glanced at his watch and told me the time. Oh well, it was only the first day.

Next morning we were taken on a guided tour of the centre of Leningrad. We visited St Isaac's cathedral, its interior sumptuously decorated with ceiling paintings, mosaics and icons. It was heavily pillared and had massive candelabra converted to electricity; before that the candle grease droppings, we were told, were carted away in wheelbarrows! As well as tourists there were many, many Russians eagerly drinking in every word that poured from the lips of the guide speaking their language, but it was strange to think that this once sacred place was now somewhere to be gawked at and not prayed in any more. Pews, if they were ever there, had been removed to make room for the shuffling thousands who passed through the building every day.

Except for the visit to St Isaac's, this was a short tour and we viewed the outside of well known buildings like the Winter Palace and the Hermitage (which we were to visit the following day). We were shown the Stock Exchange, which is a university now and proper order! At one stop for photographs the company settled into throwing snowballs, much to the amusement of passing Russians.

We rehearsed that evening at the Bolshoi Drama Theatre. The rehearsal room was fitted with a real stage, and had been since 1910! There was even a revolve – but maybe that hadn't been there since 1910. *Glasnost*, the Soviet Union's department of openness to outsiders, took care of our entertainment.

Next morning we were taken by coach to the Hermitage, only to find long queues outside; but as ever 'Intourist', that magic word, got us to the head of the line. It was a place, indeed a palace, to boast about. The very floors were works of art. Felt overshoes were provided to save the inlaid surfaces. There were massive, ornate ceilings and boulle doors of bulging beauty inside their ogee architraves. It was a tribute to the European art on display that it more than held its own in those luscious surroundings. Inlaid, veneered and carved articles of furniture vied for notice with malachite urns of the most exquisite workmanship.

There were so many items on show here, Olga our guide told us, that if one spent a minute looking at each item it would take seven years of one's life to see them all. But I think one treasures in the mind's video for replay time and time again just one item, and for me that was Van der Helst's picture of *The Family Pig Killing*. There the dead animal hangs by the hind legs down a ladder, its snout just touching the ground. Its waistcoat has been opened from tail to throat and its vitals removed. Already the children are blowing up the pig's bladder to play football, which we kids did in Kerry when Pat Murrell, the townland butcher, dispatched our pig, and for whose bloody death we children shed tears, all to be forgotten as we relished the fresh pork steaks and black pudding the following day.

We went to the Bolshoi Drama Theatre for the first showing in Russia of Tom MacIntyre's *The Great Hunger*. The cast of *The Field* assembled backstage and had coffee while waiting to be seated. Seemingly, there were no seats booked for us, and as the bell went for the start of the play we were ushered around the auditorium to any empty seats that were left. Maura and I were put sitting at the very front and we had no more than impressed our modest behinds on the seats when a gentleman and lady came to say that we were sitting in their places. What else could they have been so excited about! Fortunately, before both sides ran out of body language, an official came and took us to another part of the auditorium.

After many speeches — mercifully short, but long enough as they had to be translated into Russian — the play began. There were earphones. I put these on and there was Natasha, that gifted lady we had already met at rehearsal, interpreting the proceedings in Russian. There is much mime in *The Great Hunger*, and her task was easier than it would be in *The Field*. Tom Hickey and the cast, under Patrick Mason's splendid direction, weaved and strutted and brought to life wondrously the country people of Kavanagh's poem.

The Russians liked it and that night they gave it a standing ovation. The following evening we went to the opera at the Kirov, *Russlan and Ludmila*, a wonderful evening of music, song and a little dance, with delightful costumes and stunning scenery. Behind the dress circle was a space the size of a small theatre, a beautifully proportioned, high-ceilinged hall where patrons walked about. Boys and girls, all those good looking young people, linked and strolled, or stood and chatted under the bust of Lenin. Sainted hour, that man was everywhere, like 'that little yellow idol forever gazing down'!

We had the next day off. The stage was being set up for *The Field*. We went sightseeing to the Summer Palace of Catherine the Great. This palace, with the exception of a few rooms, was restored with infinite patience and skill after the devastation of Hitler's bombers. One never realised the full horror of the German invasion of Russia until one heard Olga, our guide, talk about the nightmare that was the siege of Leningrad. Hitler's hatred for Lenin and the Communist system was unleashed with brutal ferocity on the city and on its people. To many of them the angel of death was a welcome visitor after the demons of disease, hunger and mutilation had wreaked their worst. When I see the skeleton on the Derry coat of arms, I think of the siege of that city and I have a vision of a man frying a rat on a fire of broken furniture. Rats were eaten in Leningrad, and to survive did the people stop at that? God bless the mark. I looked into the faces of men older than myself in the streets of Leningrad and dared not think the dark thought.

Later that night we taxied to the Leningrad Hotel, a new western-type establishment with English signs everywhere. In the lettering little liberties were taken. The Russian 'C' is pronounced 'S' and restaurant appeared as 'rectaurant'. Having lived in Leningrad for four days and nearly mastered the intricacies of the Russian alphabet, I sort of resented these English intrusions as I might English signs in the gaeltacht.

On stage were the Georgian dancers, and we saw the most energetic folk dancing: high kicking of a spirited nature from the men, but the women were demure and graceful in their movements, and at no time did the men or women touch or dance in very close proximity. I can't understand why people are always praying for the conversion of Russia!

At a late dinner I had two healthy measures of vodka. Oh so smooth! But a deceptive thief; I was nearly on my ear.

Early next morning we went out for a long walk in the city. There were crowds everywhere and the footpaths were as wide as the streets. There were few cars and the architecture could be seen in relation to the human figure. The people were well fed and well dressed for the weather. They had a hankering, I was told, after the western style. Macdara

Ó Fátharta exchanged a pair of shoes for a fur hat one night. There was no litter in the streets. Hundreds would stand in a queue and when they moved (queues formed and disappeared at the drop of a hat) the street would be clean. We went to a bakery, got some lovely bread and bought milk. We made tea in our room, with bags from home, and invited Niall Tóibín in for a cuppa. He loved it, the best drop that had passed his lips since he had left Dublin. He got the radio going.

The big day arrived. We travelled by bus to the theatre at 1 p.m., settled into the dressing-rooms, donned our costumes and walked the set. We did a combined technical and dress rehearsal which went very well. It was a commodious place backstage, and there were plenty of spaces with seats where lines could be looked at. There was a full canteen service throughout the day, so there was no need to leave the theatre again.

The show started and we listened on the tannoy. That dear and gifted lady called Natasha spoke over the actors' lines and must have been near enough to the bone for the reaction was very good. Our cue coming up, Maura and I were in the wings. Cue came. We were on! I knew from the moment we hit the light that we were on the ball. The scene worked like a dream. When I burst into song at the end I transposed a line. I hope I didn't throw Natasha. It was a great night.

Afterwards the Irish ambassador came on stage. Journalists, photographers, television and radio people crowded in. It was very exciting. In high spirits we adjourned to the Hotel Europe for dinner. We had quite a night and towards morning there was a potted preview of the reviews.

On Sunday morning I went with Maura to Mass in an old church in a quiet street. It was a pre-Vatican II Latin Mass.

The celebrant's back was to us – '*féach anois mé, m'aghaidh le balla*', as the poet says – and he gave a very long sermon. The church was very full, with many people coming and going out of curiosity. Old women concerned for our comfort found seats for us. The courtesy of the people and their warmth were not like anything I had seen in a foreign country before. There were many teenagers there and children – a Russian's love for his child is pleasant to watch. With the crowds it was a bit stuffy so I went outside for a whiff of fresh air. Standing on the steps was a lady of indeterminate age who, without any preliminaries whatsoever, tried to make up to me – all very courteous and graceful, but even with the inclination, and considering my age, it wasn't the time or the place, so I took refuge within the holy walls. John Finnegan of the *Evening Herald* – older than me – told me he had had a similar experience. What these ladies won't do to get to the West!

After Mass there was a procession around the church with the Blessed Sacrament and Our Lady on a litter. Attendant children dressed in white scattered what looked like flowers in the path of the Host. As they passed, old women picked up the flowers and put the petals in their prayer books.

On the second night of *The Field* it really took off, and we got a tremendous reception at the curtain. The goodbyes to the Leningrad crew were very touching, with warm hand-shakes. The Russians are a shy people and we Irish are reserved, so there were no bear hugs.

On Monday morning we took the coach to the airport. The plane to Moscow was packed and it turned out to be a bumpy flight. The folding table kept falling down on me. There was hand luggage everywhere, and enormous Russian winter coats bulged from the overhead racks. We were in the air for an hour, and when we landed there was another hour's delay for luggage, but while the third hour was still young we were on our way to the city. There was deep snow everywhere. Trees thrust themselves out of the white plain, and in tiny groves and copses gentle birches claimed the attention, very demure and seemly in their winter nudity.

We approached the city. It was so different from Leningrad, which had been architecturally ordered. Moscow sprawled. There were plenty of open spaces. In small parks full of trees, birches again showed their pale limbs. Europe was behind us now, as we saw before us against the clouds the little domes of a cathedral looking as if an invisible angel were holding a hank of onions in the sky.

Our destination was the Russia Hotel, a modern building, part of which rose to twenty-one storeys. It was reputed to have four thousand bedrooms and it was plonked down within an ass's roar of Red Square and the fairytale-like Kremlin. Around the hotel there were many small and very lovely church-like buildings, and it seemed to me that many more must have been demolished to make room for what in this visitor's humble opinion is a monstrosity. A ground to first floor 'fly-up' roadway swept within feet of one of the picturesque churches.

In the hotel there were four entrances and reception areas, and many shops and eating places. When we got to our room, a change from Leningrad, there was so little space because of the two large beds that one of us had to remain in blanket street in the morning until the other had dressed.

That evening Mr Dara MacFhionnbháir, first secretary of the Irish embassy, gave a reception for the Abbey Company and the visiting journalists at the Godanka Restaurant. The food was excellent and my simple vegetarian requirements posed no problems. Groups of musicians entertained us, and actors and press contributed to the general hilarity. It was a great evening and a great welcome to Moscow. *Ambasáid na hÉireann, míle buíochas!*

There was a press conference at the theatre at 3 p.m. next day. Vincent Dowling came over from Dublin for the Moscow opening of *The Great Hunger*. Vladimir Cheranyean from the Ministry of Culture was there and we received a warm welcome. Vincent and Vladimir spoke, and it was mutual admiration nationwise. We heard something about the Russian theatre and especially the famous Stanislavsky Theatre we were in, but when all was almost said, there was a rift, not between the two nations, but between the Irish. A section of our press wanted to know from Vincent why these two plays had been chosen for the Abbey tour of Russia. Why not O'Casey? Or Synge? But surely Dublin, in the long months leading up to the Soviet visit, was the place to thrash this out, rather than seem to devalue what we brought in the eyes of the Russians. (If I may go into brackets for a moment, I was under the impression that the two plays we brought were the choice of the Russian Ministry of Culture, and if people ask for tea you don't give them coffee.) And one press man — the same gentleman who started the other questions — wanted to know why the plays were put on in the order in which they were presented. So much to be talked about, and time was taken up arguing as to why the football was put on before the hurling. We were embarrassed and would have welcomed a hole in the floor into which we could fall!

Mr Charles Whelan, the Irish ambassador, threw open his house to us that evening, and a fine place it was. I got a whiff of home in the shape of some reproductions from the National Gallery on the walls. My favourite was there, *The Goose Girl* by W. J. Leech, as well as a representative number of modern Irish paintings, including Noel Sheridan's *Chair*. This was a happy occasion. We met people from Aer Rianta

who were there on duty-free business, and a Russian Orthodox priest, a fine figure of a man, stood radiating charm, as
did the figure of Father Senan at the Kerrymen's meetings
when I first came to Dublin.

The next day turned out to be very interesting. A guided
tour brought us to a lovely park where the wooden palace of
Peter the Great's father once stood, and where he lived while
his stone palace was being built. There were tent-roofed
churches and buildings which housed exhibitions of artefacts
from cathedrals and palaces, an amazing collection of man's
skill in wood and metal. On the way into the park there was
a functioning Orthodox church where a service was in
progress. We mingled with the faithful, were made welcome,
and enjoyed the music, hymns, prayerful intonation, incense,
gorgeous vestments and flickering candlelight. We added to
the illumination by lighting long tapers at the shrines. I was
informed afterwards that it was a wake. A line of women in
black like Spanish widows were asking for alms and, I
supposed, praying for the dead as the old women used to do
at the holy wells when I was young.

One day I fell victim to a 'foreign tummy' and nearly
conked out. After taking some tablets Vincent O'Neill had
brought from Dublin for such an emergency, I found some
relief. I spruced up a bit later and went to the Kremlin. The
diesel they used in the tourist buses had a vile smell. Black-
blue smoke poured from the exhausts, permeated the
interior and made a bad tummy worse. We parked outside
one of the main gates. There was a long queue at the first
palace, which housed yet another museum. There were icons
by the score, which were very lovely, but like the Italian
triptychs I had seen in American galleries, they were very
much out of place away from the altars and churches for
which they were first painted. We saw vestments inlaid with

pearls and jewels, copes, mitres and croziers of a religion of yesteryear. It was like a theatre wardrobe storing costumes of a show that was not going back on stage again.

Having looked at the royal carriages that bore the tsars, I decided that as far as museums were concerned I had reached saturation point. I took leave of the party and went out in the fresh air. Two cathedrals stood within a stone's throw of each other, one of the Assumption and the other of the Annunciation. Quite near, and closer to the outer wall, was the great bulk of the CCCP government building which housed the Supreme Soviet and the Parliament of the Soviet Nations.

How beautiful the two cathedrals looked, and how varied in size, arrangement and colour those lovely domes can be in that kind of architecture. Like the icons of a while back, to me those two churches seemed a little embarrassed in their new role of museums. They missed, I would say, the incense, the chant and the gentle rhubarb of prayer. But as we had seen the other day, religion is practised in Russia. There are two kinds of churches, those that are functioning and those that are being restored. Nothing of importance is allowed to fall into disrepair. Restoration goes on apace. In fact walking the streets one notices far more reconstruction than construction. Heritage is vital in Russia.

Within the Kremlin a line not always clearly defined separates the public and government sectors, and to overstep this line brings a sharp reprimand from the police. It was my misfortune to do just that, and I have never in my life been spoken to so severely and with such venom.

I escaped to the hotel, and Des Hickey and Seamus Hosey called for me to do an interview for RTÉ radio. What better place than Red Square, and there we went and talked in the shade of Moscow's showcase piece of architecture – St Basil's

Cathedral. I don't think there is a more beautifully proportioned pile anywhere in the world. And as in the story of our own Gobán Saor, who went to build a palace for the King of England and was threatened with death, the man who fashioned this church, we are told, had his eyes put out so that he wouldn't build a better.

Snowploughs, with a great scoop in front and revolving brushes behind, kept the open space clear of snow. Red Square is a sacred — I don't know if that's the right word — place. You can't smoke there and, like the streets of Moscow and Leningrad, it was immaculately clean. There were no hoardings or advertising of any kind. No neon signs at night, just one massive red star revolving on its turret on the Kremlin wall.

Saturday was the last day for spending our roubles. We had a daily allowance from the Russians, and very grateful we were, but it had to be spent there. The time was short so an early morning shopping spree was organised. We bought what we could lay hands on while the money lasted. In the frosty street an army officer helped Maura over a slippery patch to the safety of the footpath, which was being cleared of snow by elderly women.

The Moscow Arts backstage was as big as another theatre. There were stage lifts and the stage floor tracked left and right into the wings and upstage, so that in our case after the first scene, the 'pub' set glided left and the 'field' set came in from the right. If we needed a third set, the 'field' could move right and another scene could roll in from upstage. All this equipment, together with the flies, made for what must be a director's dream. But what impressed me most was the space. I love space, having worked in the most awful cramped conditions touring around Ireland.

There was a hint of nerves on opening night, but despite

this the piece played well. Natasha had made her own of the text, and the reaction right through was just as if we were in Dublin. To sit in a Russian audience, as we did on our nights off, and to be part of their involvement in what goes on on stage was an experience. Soul, as it were, reached out to soul. We were lucky to experience that total involvement from the other side of the footlights. What must it have been like for the actors and the spectators when the great Chekhovian plays were first presented in this hallowed place.

At the curtain the house came down. We all felt we wanted to say: 'We love you! Thanks a million!' and Niall Tóibín, stepping forward, did just that, very gracefully and in Russian, ending with '*Spaseeba! Spaseeba! Bolshoi spaseeba!*'

Sunday morning, 21 February, we were all set to go to the circus, but at the last moment tickets became available for the Bolshoi Theatre. We opted for the ballet, myself a little sadly, being an old circus fan, and it also meant that I missed my last chance of riding the Moscow Metro that everyone talks about. We went off then in great glee to the Bolshoi to find that it was 'opera morning': not seeing the world famous ballet on its home ground was a disappointment.

The Bolshoi Theatre's classic exterior, with an equine group dashing forth from above the apex of the tympanum, was but a foretaste of the theatre inside, cathedral-like in its majesty, with a great proscenium opening and a hammer-and-sickle patterned curtain. A loge skirted the entire wall and five balconies were shelved up along the side walls, with a huge box centre back and two other boxes, one on either side of the stage. Everything was decorated and gilded and there was a painted ceiling. In such beautiful and pains-takingly restored theatres I felt that the drama, ballet and opera had taken the place of religion. The people were streaming in this bright Sunday morning when devout parishioners in Listowel were pounding the flags to Mass.

We nearly overslept the day we went home. Martin Fahy rang just as the porters were calling for our luggage at 4.15 a.m. Luckily the two large bags had been packed since the previous night. We had a hectic half hour to get ready and appear down at the exit. We made it. John Costigan had our passports and tickets and more forms to fill — currency declarations and again the old questions. Any weapons? Any ammunition? Any antiques? No! But there were many sore heads after our last night in Moscow and only a few hours in bed. The porter pressed a Lenin badge into my palm and I pressed some roubles into his. Eventually we were in the coach and had a long drive through the falling snow and Moscow's sleeping suburbs. Snowploughs driving at a furious rate cleared the roads to the airport.

The customs, even with the help of the kindly *glasnost* girls, turned out to be very slow. And judging by the scrutiny and long delay at the passport counter, it's no cakewalk getting out of Russia. We were shepherded from pen to pen and finally our bags went off, jauntily I felt, along the conveyor belt, as anxious as ourselves to be going home. Then came a surprise, a very welcome breakfast from our hosts, and in no time we were on our Aeroflot plane bound for Leningrad. The trip took an hour, an hour's wait, and then the high skies to Shannon.

We were not allowed off the plane at Leningrad, and we sat out the hour on the runway. Sixty to a hundred college boys and their teachers from St Fintan's High School in Sutton joined us there. It sounded like home already as youthful Irish voices were raised in every section of the plane. We took off at 10.10 a.m. It's a three-hour trip, and Ireland is three hours behind in time. We raced the sun but never beat it. It cast the same shadow in Shannon as it had in Leningrad.

Another shadow fell. And our spirits sagged a little. On picking up the Irish morning papers we found that the summing up of our historic visit to the Soviet Union was greatly at variance with our collective experience.

We were home!

26

ALONE IN THE MOTHER HOUSE

In October 1990 I took part in a Sense of Ireland week in London. I played in the Riverside Studio at Hammersmith. Out walking from the hotel the night before, I lost my way. I called to a man in front and when he heard my voice he quickened his step. Then he stopped and, turning back, he asked me if I was Éamon Kelly. We walked along and went into a pub, and he told me that when he was a youngster in rural Ireland his job was to stand at the kitchen door and, when I came on the radio in *The Rambling House*, to call his mother, who was milking the cows, to hear me.

It was strange, he said, hearing my voice in a London street. At first he thought it was a ghost, which was why he had hastened his step. He told me that his mother and the people of her generation wouldn't miss me on the radio for anything. He turned his head and, gazing past me, he said, 'I was home to her funeral only last week.'

Next morning bright and early I was at the Riverside Studio. Michael Doyle had come over from the Abbey with me, and my set and stage furniture had been shipped across. We set up the scene and in the afternoon while I was resting Michael lit it. That night we opened. There was a great crowd.

I always manage to draw a hearty laugh in the first minute. It relaxes them. When I was telling the story of Father McGillicuddy and the first motor car seen in our parish, an almighty clap of thunder broke directly overhead. I waited, looking up into the flies until the noise was dying away, and then I said, 'God is getting vexed with me!' The house came down.

Maura and I stayed at the Tara Hotel where we were made very welcome by my friend Eoin Dillon the manager. Bosco Hogan was there. His show *I am Ireland*, about W. B. Yeats was coming into the Riverside Studio after me. We ran into Brian Friel and Patrick Mason. Brian's play *Dancing at Lughnasa* was opening in the National the next week.

After the run, when I came back to Dublin, Noel Pearson, the then artistic director of the Abbey, asked me to see him. The current play in the theatre had opened to the father and mother of a lambasting from the critics. The stalls were practically empty. Would I take over with my one-man show at the Abbey for a few weeks?

It was a tall order and at first nearly knocked the wind out of me. It was all right doing a one-man show in the Peacock, in London or America, but the Abbey – the sacred stomping ground of poets and playwrights! Then I said to myself, what the heck? I had a show fresh in my mind and if it did well in London it should do better in the Abbey.

The name of the one-man show was *English That for Me*, about the time when Irish was being supplanted by the foreign tongue in my native place. It had the heartbreak, the high comedy and the misunderstandings of such a set of circumstances.

Maura encouraged me to go ahead, though my son Brian said I was taking on too much at seventy-six. I did it. Some nights I was put to the pin of my collar to keep going, but strength came after a plea went skywards to relieve me in my hardest hour, and I kept the doors of the Abbey open until Field Day took over with *The Cure at Troy* by Seamus Heaney.

As someone reminded me, I had made a little bit of history that night. I was the first Abbey actor to do a one-man show in the mother house.

It was after Noel Pearson that Garry Hynes came to us as artistic director. Being away from the theatre quite a bit, I didn't figure in too many of her shows, though she did nearly put a halt to my gallop as an actor by miscasting me as Uncle Peter in her ever so controversial production of *The Plough and the Stars*. I refused to do the part when approached, but she got round me. After the first reading of the play I kicked over the traces when I saw that it wasn't working for me. I came home and wrote two letters; one to Martin Fahy the theatre manager, tendering my resignation from the company, and the other to Garry Hynes to the effect that I didn't feel happy in the part. I was going out the door to put the letters in the post when the phone rang. It was Garry, and I'll say this much for her, for a small parcel of humanity she is mighty persuasive. She talked me out of the decision I had made by dint of praise and cajolery.

On opening night, in a cast of shaved heads and some tongues with vague echoes of Belfast, Galway and west Munster, maybe I wasn't entirely out of place. There were Dubliners on stage too, but ne'er a sign of a faded Georgian casement or arched doorway to give the tang of a tenement house. Mollser the consumptive child sat at the corner of a raked stage catching the sun with a mug in her hand.

'Mollser, oul' son. What are you drinkin'? Milk?'
'Grand, Fluther. Grand thanks. Tis milk.'
'You couldn't get a bether thing down you.'

Furniture brought on to the same space gave the effect of an interior. The setting was very different from those of the O'Casey plays we had seen down the years. Old-timers hated the production and *The Irish Times* nearly had a fit. But there were many who loved Garry's very different look at the great man's work, with the stress on poverty and on suffering.

At rehearsals, when I settled down to accepting my role as Uncle Peter, I enjoyed working with Garry. She was often inspired and always inspiring, and the Holy Ghost descended on her many times during the weeks of preparation. She didn't believe in leaving well alone. Frank O'Connor once told me that he could never re-read even his best short story without wanting to change it. That same itch for change motivated Garry. When she had set a scene, if you went to the loo, you came back to find it completely altered. Where before you had entered from the stair landing, you now came up through a trap-door in the floor, as the auxiliaries did in *The Plough and the Stars*. You could never be up to her.

In our last play together, which was *The Colleen Bawn* at the Royal Exchange in Manchester, Myles na Gopaleen descended from the flies to land on the lake shore in Killarney! Playing Father Tom, the *poitín* priest in *The Colleen Bawn*, and watching the plot develop, I couldn't help thinking that in many ways John B. Keane was heir to Boucicault. As in John B.'s plays, Boucicault's characters are colourful and his dialogue comes trippingly off the tongue. *The Colleen Bawn* is set by the lakes of Killarney, and for me who was born near there the language of Boucicault, though not as authentic as that of Keane, is racy the soil.

That's my story. My journeying is over. I am eighty-four and my next trek will be through the stars to the great beyond, where I hope to meet again those I knew in my wanderings down here: those with whom I shared the craftsman's bench, those who taught me and those I taught in my spell in the classroom, those whose voices rode the radio waves with mine, and finally those with whom I strutted my merry hour upon the stage.

If the humour takes us and there's a playwright handy, Hilton Edwards or the Abbey's Frank Dermody may be tempted to direct a show in some celestial alhambra, where angels with folded wings will sit in the stalls, applaud politely and maybe come round after and say, 'That was great!'

INDEX